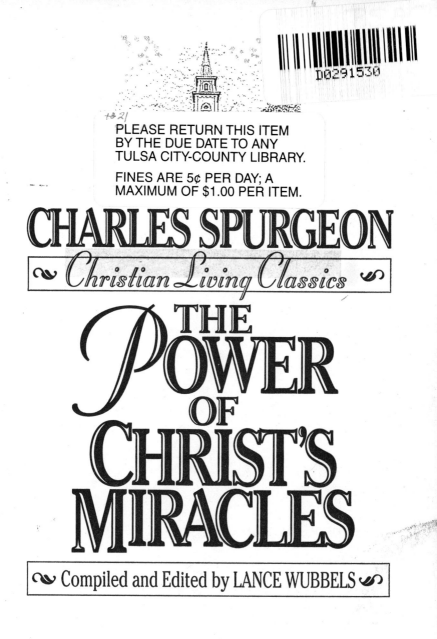

CHARLES SPURGEON

Christian Living Classics

THE POWER OF CHRIST'S MIRACLES

Compiled and Edited by LANCE WUBBELS

Emerald Books

P.O. Box 635 • Lynnwood, Washington 98046

Scripture quotations are taken from the King James Version of the Bible.

To
David Koechel

"I have filled him with the Spirit of God,
with skill, ability and knowledge
in all kinds of crafts—to make artistic designs
for work in gold, silver and bronze,
to cut and set stones, to work in wood,
and to engage in all kinds of craftsmanship."

CHARLES SPURGEON
CHRISTIAN LIVING CLASSICS

Grace Abounding in a Believer's Life

A Passion for Holiness in a Believer's Life

The Power of Christ's Miracles

The Power of Prayer in a Believer's Life

Spiritual Warfare in a Believer's Life

The Triumph of Faith in a Believer's Life

What the Holy Spirit Does in a Believer's Life

About the Editor

LANCE WUBBELS is the managing editor of Bethany House Publishers. His interest in the writings of Charles Spurgeon began while doing research on an editorial project that required extensive reading of Spurgeon's sermons. He discovered a wealth of sermon classics that are filled with practical, biblical insight for every believer and written in a timeless manner that makes them as relevant today as the day they were spoken. His desire is to select and present Spurgeon's writings in a way that will appeal to a wide audience of readers and allow one of the greatest preachers of all time to enrich believers' lives.

Wubbels is also the author of The Gentle Hills fiction series with Bethany House Publishers, a heartwarming series that is set during World War II. A naturally gifted storyteller, he captures readers with a warm, homey style filled with wit and insight that appeals to a wide readership.

About the Author

CHARLES HADDON SPURGEON (1834–1892) was the remarkable British "Boy Preacher of the Fens" who became one of the truly greatest preachers of all time. Coming from a flourishing country pastorate in 1854, he accepted a call to pastor London's New Park Street Chapel. This building soon proved too small and so work on Spurgeon's Metropolitan Tabernacle was begun in 1859. Meanwhile his weekly sermons were being printed and having a remarkable sale—25,000 copies every week in 1865 and translated into more than twenty languages.

Spurgeon built the Metropolitan Tabernacle into a congregation of over 6,000 and added well over 14,000 members during his thirty-eight-year London ministry. The combination of his clear voice, his mastery of language, his sure grasp of Scripture, and a deep love for Christ produced some of the noblest preaching of any age. An astounding 3,561 sermons have been preserved in sixty-three volumes, *The New Park Street Pulpit* and *The Metropolitan Tabernacle Pulpit,* from which the chapters of this book have been selected and edited.

During his lifetime, Spurgeon is estimated to have preached to 10,000,000 people. He remains history's most widely read preacher. There is more available material written by Spurgeon than by any other Christian author, living or dead. His sixty-three volumes of sermons stand as the largest set of books by a single author in the history of Christianity, comprising the equivalent to the twenty-seven volumes of the ninth edition of the *Encyclopedia Britannica.*

Contents

Introduction

THE AMAZING SUCCESS of Charles Haddon Spurgeon's thirty-eight-year metropolitan ministry in the city of London during the second half of the nineteenth century was said to have been unparalleled in England since the days of George Whitefield and John Wesley. During nearly four decades of ministry, he built London's Metropolitan Tabernacle into the world's largest independent congregation and established a preaching legacy that may never be surpassed. Those decades of ministry remain one of the greatest pastoral, evangelistic, social ministries ever seen.

Recognized by his peers then and now as "The Prince of Preachers," it is also remarkable that Spurgeon remains history's most widely read preacher. There is more available material written by Spurgeon than by any other Christian author, living or dead, and his sixty-three volumes of sermons stand as the largest set of books by a single author in the history of Christianity. The sermons are passionate, rich in biblical insight, understandable, and so practical that one cannot help but be inspired and challenged. It's no wonder they are read constantly.

Being a wonderfully visual expositor, Spurgeon preached a remarkable number of sermons that centered around the miracles of Jesus Christ. His word pictures of the many colorful individuals to whom Christ brought healing and the events where Christ may have calmed the seas or fed the five thousand represent a powerful storytelling skill that gripped his listeners' hearts. With so many Spurgeon messages on the miracles available, selecting twelve of the best was no simple task.

Journey then with Charles Spurgeon as he paints the biblilcal scenery of some of Christ's most stunning miracles. Read about the poor victim who had waited at the pool of Bethesda for thirty-eight years and about whom Spurgeon says Christ selected as "the worst case to be dealt with by His curing hand as a type of what He often does in the kingdom of grace, and as a lesson of prudence to us, instructing us to give our first aid to those who are first in point of need." Consider with Spurgeon the leper, whose disease had left him lost and hopeless, or behold the blind beggar who refused to be quieted when he heard that Jesus Christ was passing his way.

Spurgeon believed that "the object of the miracles is to reveal more fully the power and authority of our Lord's Word and to let us see by signs following that His teaching has an omnipotent force about it. This truth is much needed at the present moment, for if the gospel does not still save men, if it is not still 'the power of God unto salvation to every one that believeth' (Rom. 1:16), then the attacks of skepticism are not easily repelled. But if the gospel is still a thing of power over the minds of men, a power conquering sin and Satan, let them say what they like, our only answer shall be to lament their doubts and to scorn their scorning. Oh, for an hour of the Son of man! Oh, where is He that trod the sea and bade the rage of hell subside with a word?"

And the splendor of miracles of Christ is not limited to what they teach us about the power of Christ to rescue us from sin. It is also clear from many of the miracles that the simplest action of life may be sublimely great. Spurgeon says that when Peter let down his net at Jesus' word after having caught nothing all night that "the flash of the wave as it covers Peter's net may be as sublime before the Lord as the glory of the Red Sea billow when it returned in its strength. God who sees a world in a drop sees wonders in the smallest act of faith. Do not, I pray you, think that sublimity lies in masses, to be measured in a scale, so that a mile shall be sublime and an inch shall be absurd. We measure not moral and spiritual things by rods and chains."

You have to love how Spurgeon brought the Word of God to the hearts of his listeners and readers. Listen to Spurgeon's plea as he relates the story of the leper to our lives: "Hear me, O trembling sinner: if you are as full of sin as an egg is full of meat, Jesus can remove it all. If your propensities to sin are as untameable as the wild boar of the wood, yet Jesus Christ, the Lord of all, can subdue your iniquities and make you the obedient servant of His love. Jesus can turn the lion into a lamb, and He can do it now. He can transform you where you are sitting, saving you while you read this word. All things are possible to the Savior God, and all things are possible to him who believes."

I invite you to read these select chapters as you would listen to a trusted and skilled pastor, for that is what Spurgeon was. There is nothing speculative about Spurgeon's teaching; just the rock-solid truth. Spurgeon will meet you where you live, and you will not be disappointed.

Careful editing has helped to sharpen the focus of these sermons while retaining the authentic and timeless flavor they undoubtedly bring.

The Church of God on earth at this present time anxiously desires to spread her influence over the world. For Christ's sake we wish to have the truths we preach acknowledged and the precepts that we deliver obeyed. But mark, no church will ever have power over the masses of this or any other land except in proportion as she does them good. The day has long since passed in which any church may hope to prevail on the plea of history. "Look at what we were," is a vain appeal: men only care for what we are. The church that glorifies itself with the faded laurels of past centuries and is content to be inactive today is near to its inglorious end.

Chapter One

The Work of Grace,
the Warrant for Obedience

He that made me whole, the same said unto me, Take up thy bed,
and walk—John 5:11.

JUST A FEW OBSERVATIONS upon the narrative itself. It was a feast day, and Jesus Christ came up to Jerusalem to find opportunities for doing good among the crowds of His countrymen. I see all the city glad. I can hear the voice of rejoicing in every house as they hold high festival and eat the fat and drink the sweet. But where does Jesus keep the feast? How does He spend His holiday? He walks among the poor, whom He loves so well.

Behold Him in the hospital. There was one notable Bethesda or "house of mercy" in Jerusalem. It was a poor provision for the city's abounding sickness, but such as it was it was greatly prized. There was a pool that every now and then was stirred by an angel's wing and wrought an occasional cure. Around it charitable persons had built five porches, and there on the cold stone steps a number of blind and lame and withered folk were lying, each one upon his own wretched pallet, waiting for the moving of the waters. There were the weary children of pain, fainting while others were feasting, racked with pain amid general rejoicing, sighing amid universal singing.

Our Lord was at home amid this mercy, for here was room for His tender heart and powerful hand. He feasted His soul by doing good. Let us learn this lesson, dear friend, that in the times of our brightest joys we should remember the sorrowful and find a still higher joy in doing them good. In proportion as a day is joyous to ourselves, it is good to make it so to the sick and poor around us. Let us keep the feast by sending portions to those for whom nothing is prepared, lest the famishing may bring a curse upon our feasting. When we prosper in business, let us set aside a portion for the poor. When we are full of health and strength, let us remember those to whom these privileges are denied and aid those who minister to them. Blessed shall they be who, like the Lord Jesus, visit the sick and care for them.

Coming into the hospital, our Lord noticed a certain man whose case was a very sad one. There were many painful cases there, but Jesus singled out this man, and it would seem that the reason for His choice was that the poor creature was in the worst plight of all. If misery has a claim on pity, then the greater the sufferer, the more is mercy attracted toward him. This poor victim of rheumatism or paralysis had been thirty-eight years bound by his infirmity. Let us hope that there was no worse case in all Bethesda's porches! Thirty-eight years is more than half the appointed period of human life. One year of pain or paralysis has a weary length of torture about it, but think of thirty-eight! We may well pity the man who endures the pangs of rheumatism even for an hour, but how shall we sufficiently pity him who has not been free from it for nearly forty years? Even if the case were one not of pain but of paralysis, the inability to work and the consequent poverty of so many years were by no means a small evil. Our Lord, then, selects the worst case to be dealt with by His curing hand as a type of what He often does in the kingdom of grace and as a lesson of prudence to us, instructing us to give our first aid to those who are first in point of need.

The man whom Jesus healed was by no means an attractive character. Our Savior said to him when he was healed, "Sin no more, lest a worse thing come unto thee," from which it is not an improbable inference that his first infirmity had come upon him by some deed of vice or course of excess. The man apparently had been guilty of that which brought upon his body the suffering that he was enduring. It is considered generally to be a point beyond all dispute that we should help the worthy but should refuse the worthless—that when a man brings a calamity upon himself by wrongdoing, we are justified in letting him suffer, that he may reap what he has sown. This cold Pharisaic idea is very congenial to minds that are bent upon saving their money. It springs up in many hearts—or rather in places where hearts should be—and it is generally regarded as if it were a rule of prudence that is beyond dispute, an axiom infallible and universal.

I venture to say that our Savior never taught us to confine our giving to the deserving. He would never have bestowed His grand gift of grace on any one of us had He carried out that rule. We cannot afford to cramp our charity into a sort of petty justice and sour our giving into a miniature court of law. When a man is suffering, let us pity him, however the suffering has come. When a man has been in misery so long as thirty-eight years, it is time that his infirmity should be more considered than his iniquity and that his present sorrow should be thought upon more than his former folly. So Jesus thought, and therefore He came to the sinner, not with reproach but with restoration. Jesus saw his disease rather than his depravity and gave him pity instead of punishment.

Our God is kind to the unthankful and to the evil; be therefore merciful, as your Father also is merciful. Remember how our Lord said, "Pray for them which despitefully use you, and persecute you; That ye may be the children of your Father which is in heaven: for he maketh his sun to rise on the evil and on the good, and sendeth rain on the just and on the unjust" (Matt. 5:44-45). Let us imitate Him in this, and wherever there is pain and sorrow, let it be our joy to relieve it.

In addition to the supposition that this man had at some time been grossly guilty, it seems clear from the text that he was a poor, shiftless, discouraged, depressed sort of person. He had never managed to get into the pool, though others had done so who were as infirm as he. He had never been able to win a friend or secure a helper, though from the extreme length of his infirmity, one would have thought that at some period or another he might have found a man to place him in the pool when the angel gave it the mystic stir. The Savior's asking him, "Wilt thou be made whole?" (John 5:6), leads us to think that he had fallen into such a listless, despairing, heartsick condition that though he came daily to the edge of the pool as a matter of habit, he not only had ceased to hope but also had almost ceased to wish. Our Lord touched the chord that was most likely to respond—namely, the man's will and desire to be made whole—but the response was a very feeble one. The man's answer shows what a poor creature he was, for there is not a beam of hope in it, or even of desire. It is more of a wail, a hopeless dirge, a grievous complaint: "I have no man, when the water is troubled, to put me into the pool: but while I am coming, another steppeth down before me" (John 5:7).

The utter imbecility and lack of brain of the poor creature is most seen in the fact that like a simpleton he went to Christ's enemies and told them that it was Jesus who had made him whole. I am sure there was no malice in his informing our Lord's enemies, for had there been, he would have said, "It was Jesus who bade me take up my bed," whereas he worded it thus: "It was Jesus, which had made [me] whole" (John 5:15).

I hardly dare, however, to hope, as some do, that there was much gratitude about this testimony, though doubtless the poor soul was grateful. I would suppose that his long endurance of pain, acting upon a weak mind, had brought him to an almost imbecile state of mind, so that he spoke without thought. Our Lord did not, therefore, require much of him. Jesus did not ask even for a distinct avowal of faith from him, but asked only for that small measure of it that might be implied in his answering the question, "Wilt thou be made whole?" This poor man did not show any of the shrewdness of the man born blind, who answered the Pharisees so keenly; he was of quite another type and could do no more than state his own case to Jesus. Thank God, even that was enough for our Lord to work with. The Lord Jesus saves people of all sorts. He has among His disciples men of quick and ready wit who can baffle their opponents, but quite as often He chooses a poor simpleton of a creature and works a great marvel upon him to the exceeding praise of His condescending grace.

Note well that this man's mind, though there was not much of it, was all engrossed and filled up with the fact that he had been made whole. Jesus to him was He that made him whole. Of the person of Jesus he knew next to nothing, for he had seen Him for only an instant, and then he did not know that it was Jesus. His one idea of Jesus was, "He that made me whole." This was natural in his case, and it will be equally natural in our own. Even when the saved ones are more intelligent than this poor paralytic, they must still chiefly think of the Son of God as their Savior who made them whole. I may not know much about the Lord, yet I do know that He has saved me. I was burdened with guilt and full of woes and could not rest day or night until He gave me peace. I may not be able to tell another much concerning the glory of His person, His attributes, His relationships, His offices, or His work, yet I can say, "One thing I know...whereas I was blinded by error, now I see; whereas I was paralyzed by sin, I am now able to stand upright and walk in His ways."

This poor soul knew the Lord experientially, and that is the best way of knowing Him. Actual contact with Him yields a surer and a truer knowledge than all the reading in the world. In the kingdom of Christ, wonderful facts transpire, such as conversion and finding peace with God, and happy are they to whom these facts are personal experiences. When men are turned from the error of their ways and when their heart finds rest and peace in Christ, great deeds are done by the Lord Jesus. If you are acquainted with these two things, even though you should be ignorant of a great deal else, be not afraid of exaggerating their importance, but set your mind on them and call Jesus by that name—"He that made me whole." Think of Him under that aspect, and you will have a very valuable and influential idea of Him. You shall see greater things than these, but for the present, let these happy and sure facts be much upon your mind, even as his being made whole was upon this man's mind.

As for the cavilling Pharisees, you observe that they took no notice of the glorious fact of the man's cure. They willfully ignored what Christ had done but fell full swoop upon that little, insignificant circumstance that it had been done on the Sabbath day, and then they spent all their thoughts and emotions upon that side issue. They say nothing of the man's being restored, but they rage because the man carried his bed on the Sabbath. It is much the same with the men of the world today. They habitually ignore the fact of conversion; if they do not deny it, they look upon it as being a matter not worth caring about. Although they see the harlot made chaste, and the thief made honest, and the profane made devout, and the despairing made joyful, and other moral and spiritual changes of the utmost practical value, they forget all this and attack some peculiar point of doctrine or mode of speech or diversity of manner and raise a storm concerning these. Is it because the facts themselves, if fairly looked at, would establish what they do not care to believe? They persistently forget the fact that Christianity is doing marvels in this world, such as nothing else ever did, but that fact is just what you and I must as persistently remember. We must dwell upon what Christ by His Holy Spirit has wrought within our nature by renewing us in the spirit of our minds, and we must make this work of grace a fountain of argument that will establish our faith and justify our conduct. This poor man did so. He did not know much else, but that he had been made whole he did know, and from that fact he justified himself in what he had done: "He that made me whole, the same said unto me, take up thy bed and walk."

This is the truth that I want to enlarge upon. First, by saying that the work of Christ furnishes us with *a justification for our obedience to His command*—"He that made me whole, the same said unto me"—that is our complete justification for what we do. In the second place, the work of Jesus Christ throws upon us *an obligation to do what He bids us*—if He that made me whole says to me, take up your bed and walk, I am bound to do it, and I should feel the obligation of His goodness pressing upon me. In the third place, not only is it a justification and an obligation, but the deed of grace becomes *a constraint to obedience*—He who said to me, "Rise," and so made me whole, by that same word of power made me take up my bed and walk. The power that saves us also moves us to obey our Savior. Not with our own might do we fulfill the will of our Lord, but with the power that the Healer gives us in the selfsame hour. May the Holy Spirit lead us into the power of this truth, for I am persuaded that a sense of the Lord's work within us is a great force and should be excited and applied to the highest ends.

A Justification for Our Obedience to His Command

This poor man could not defend the action of taking up his bed and walking, for his enemies were experts in the law and he was not. You and I could defend it very easily, for it seems to us a very proper thing to do under the circumstances. The weight of his bed was not much more than that of an ordinary winter coat. It was a simple rug or mat upon which he was lying. There really was no violation of God's law of the Sabbath, and therefore there was nothing to excuse. But the rabbis laid down rules of which I will give you but one example—"It is unlawful to carry a handkerchief loose in the pocket." But if you pin it to your pocket or tie it around your waist as a belt, you may carry it anywhere because it becomes a part of your dress. To my unsophisticated mind it would have seemed that the pin increased the ponderous burden, and so increased the weight to be carried more than was necessary! This was quite a weighty business according to rabbinical estimates.

Most of the rabbinical regulations with regard to the Sabbath were absolutely ludicrous, but this poor man was not in a position to say so or even to think so, for, like the rest of his countrymen, he stood in awe of the scribes and doctors. These learned Pharisees and priests were too much reverenced for this poor creature to answer them in their own manner. But he did what you and I must always do when we are at all puzzled—he hid behind the Lord Jesus and pleaded, "He that made me whole, the same said unto me, take up thy bed." That was quite enough for him, and he quoted it as if he felt that it was enough for those who questioned him. Truly it should have been so. I may not be able to find in my own knowledge and ability an authority equal to the authority of learned unbelievers, but my personal experience of the power of grace will stand me in as good a stead as this man's cure was to him. He argued that there must be in the man who made him whole enough authority to match the greatest possible rabbi who ever lived. Even his poor, feeble mind could grasp that, and surely you and I may do the same—we can defend ourselves behind the breastplate of our Savior's gracious work and the consequent authority that belongs to Him.

There are certain *ordinances* to which a Christian man is bound to attend about which the world raises a storm of questions. The world does not take notice that a man was once a drunkard and has through divine grace become sober and so has become a good father and a good husband and a good citizen. It lets that miracle pass by unheeded, but when the man is going to be baptized, they at once object to the ordinance. Or he is going to join a Christian church, and straightway they jeer at him as a Presbyterian or a Methodist, as if it matters what sort of name they give him so long as he is a better man than themselves and is redeemed from sin and taught to be upright and chaste and pure in the sight of God. The work of grace goes for nothing with them, but just the peculiarity of the denomination or the peculiarity of the ordinance is made a world of. These are blind creatures who despise the medicine that heals because of the bottle that contains it or the label by which it is named. However, our answer is, "He that made us whole," the same gave us a command, and by that command we will abide.

We seek no justification but this, that He who wrought a miracle of grace upon us bade us do it. What if I am about to be baptized as a believer, the same that said "Believe" said "Be baptized." He who gave me salvation also said, "He that believeth and is baptized shall be saved" (Mk. 16:16). Over against all objections we set the divine authority of Jesus. He by whose blood we are cleansed and by whose Spirit we are renewed is Lord and lawgiver to us. His precept is our sufficient warrant. If we go to the communion table and revilers say, "What is the use of eating a piece of bread and drinking a drop of wine? Why think so solemnly of so small a matter?", we reply that He who made us whole also said, "This do in remembrance of me" (1 Cor. 11:24). We renounce what He has not ordained, but we cling to His statutes. If He had commanded a ceremony still more open to objection in the eyes of carnal man, we would make no further apology than this: He who has created us anew and given us a hope of heaven and led us to seek after perfect holiness, He has bid us do it. This is our final reply, and although we could find other justifications, they would be superfluous. Stand that for our defense—the Savior commands.

The same apology applies to all *the doctrines* of the gospel. I say again, ungodly men will not admit—or if they admit it, they ignore it—that the gospel works a marvelous change in men's hearts. If they want proof, we can find them instances by hundreds and thousands of the reclaiming, elevating, and purifying power of the gospel of Jesus Christ. The gospel is daily working spiritual miracles, but this they forget, and they go on to find fault with its peculiar doctrines. Justification by faith they frequently quarrel with. "Well now," they say, "that is a shocking doctrine. If you teach men that they are to be saved by faith alone and not by their works, of course they will lead loose lives. If you continually declare that salvation is of grace alone and not of merit, the inevitable result will be that men will sin that grace may abound." We find a complete answer to this calumny in the fact that believers in justification by faith and in the doctrines of grace are among the best and purest of men and that as a fact, these truths work holiness.

But we do not care to argue this point. We prefer to remind our adversaries that He who has caused us to be regenerate men Himself taught us that whoever believes in Him shall be saved, expressly declaring that He who believes in Him has everlasting life. By the mouth of His servant Paul, He has said that by grace are men saved through faith, and that not of themselves, it is the gift of God (Eph. 2:8). He has also told us that by the works of the law shall no flesh be justified, and He has bid us declare that "the just shall live by faith" (Gal. 3:11). He who is daily by His gospel turning men from sin to holiness has given this for the sum total of the gospel we are to preach: "Look unto me, and be ye saved, all the ends of the earth" (Isa. 45:22). If this gospel does not make men better and change their evil natures, you may question it if you like. But while it continues its purifying work, we shall not blush or stammer when we declare the doctrines that are its essence and life. Our regeneration proves to us our Lord's authority, and upon that we are prepared to base our creed. To us the best of evidence is His work within us, and in that evidence we place implicit faith.

The same applies to all *the precepts* that the Christian is called upon to obey. For instance, if he is true to the faith, the believer keeps himself from all the sinful pleasures, practices, and policies of the world in which others take delight. Consequently, the ungodly world says that he is singular, precise, and self-opinionated. This is the answer for all Christians: "He who made us whole, the same said to us, ye are not of the world, even as I am not of the world. Come ye out from among them and be ye separate. Touch not the unclean thing, and I will receive you." If you follow the precepts of the Lord Jesus Christ, you may meet all charges of singularity by urging the supremacy of the Savior, whose power has made you a new creature. Where His word is, there is a power to which we bow at once. It is ours not to question our Savior but to obey Him. We are cleansed by His blood, we are redeemed by His death, and we live by His life, and therefore we are not ashamed to take up His cross and follow Him.

This apology should suffice even those who oppose us, for if they felt as grateful as we do, they would obey also. They ought at any rate to say, "We cannot blame these men for doing as Jesus bids them, because He has done so much for them." Surely the poor man who had been thirty-eight years paralyzed could not be blamed for obeying the command of one who in a moment restored him to health and strength. If he became Jesus' servant for life, who would censure him? Should not such a benefactor exert a boundless influence over him? What could be more natural and proper?

Unconverted people must excuse us if we, in obedience to our Lord Jesus, do many things that seem very singular, for though we would not needlessly offend, we cannot please others at the risk of displeasing our Lord. We do not owe so much to the whole world as we owe to the Lord Jesus; in fact, truth to tell, we do not feel that we owe anything to the world. The time past is sufficient for us to have wrought the will of the Gentiles, for when we are asked the question, "What fruit had ye then in those things whereof ye are now ashamed?" (Rom. 6:21), we have to confess that we had no fruit except the sour grapes that set our teeth on edge. Like the shipmen who put out to sea against Paul's advice, our only gain has been loss and damage. In serving the world we found the labor weariness and the wages death. But as for our Lord Jesus, we owe Him everything, and so you must excuse us if we try to follow Him in everything.

It seems to us that this is an excuse that should be accepted from us as covering the whole ground, but if it is refused, we are not at all dismayed, for it quite suffices us—yes, more than suffices us, it makes us glory in what we do. Does Jesus command? Then it is ours to obey. Objectors may say concerning one of His ordinances, it is unsuitable to the climate, it is indecent, it is needless, it is I do not know what. All this is no concern of ours; if Jesus bade us do it, His command stands for us in the place of reasoning. He who made us whole gives us sufficient excuse for obedience in that very fact. "Oh, but it is contrary to what the fathers teach and to what the church teaches." We care not the snap of our fingers for all the fathers and all the churches under heaven if they go contrary to what our Lord teaches, for they did not make us whole, and we are not under obligation to them as we are to Him. The authority of Jesus is supreme because it is from His lips that we received the word that healed the sickness of our sin. This satisfies our conscience now, and it will do so amid the solemnities of death. How can we make a mistake if we follow the words of Jesus in all things? We can plead His precept as our warrant at the last great day, before the Judge of quick and dead. What better plea can we have than this: "Thou didst make us whole and thou didst bid us do this"? Such a justification of our conduct will make our death pillow soft and our resurrection bright with joy.

Instead of admitting that this is not an ample justification, let us go further still in the strength of it. If the world has accounted us vile for obeying our Lord, let us be viler still. And inasmuch as He who made us whole said, "Go ye into all the world, and preach the gospel to every creature" (Mk. 16:15), let us endeavor to spread abroad everywhere the savor of His name, consecrating ourselves body, soul, and spirit to the extension of His kingdom. He who made us whole will make the world whole yet by His own wondrous power. Have we not abundantly shown that our Lord's command is a solid justification of our conduct?

The Cure Brought Forth an Obligation

"He that made me whole, the same said unto me, Take up thy bed, and walk." The argument takes this form. First, He who made me whole is divine, or He could not do this miracle; or, to say the least, He must be divinely authorized. And if He is divine, or divinely authorized, I must be bound to obey the orders He issues. Is not that a plain argument that even the poor, simple mind of the paralytic man was able to grasp and wield? Let us try to feel the force of that argument ourselves. Jesus who has saved us is our God; shall we not obey Him? Since He is clothed with divine power and majesty, shall we not scrupulously endeavor to know His will and zealously endeavor to carry it out at every point, as His Spirit shall enable us?

In addition to the divine character that the miracle proved and displayed, there was the goodness that shone in the deed of power and touched the poor man's heart. His argument was "I *must* do what my great Deliverer bids me. How can you think otherwise? Did He not make me whole? Would you have *me*, whom He has thus graciously restored, refuse to fulfill His desire? Must I not take up my bed the moment He gives me strength to do it? How can I do otherwise? Is this to be the recompense I pay to my good Physician, at once to refuse to do what He asks of me? Do you not see that I am under an obligation that it would be shameful to deny? He restores these limbs, and I am bound to do with them what He orders me do with them. He says 'Walk,' and since these once withered feet have been restored, shall I not walk? He bids me roll up my bed, and since I could not have used my hands till just now, His word gave them life, shall I not use them to roll up the bed-rug at His bidding? These poor shoulders of mine were bent with weakness, but He has made me stand upright, and since He now bids me carry my bed, shall I not throw the mattress on my shoulders and bear the easy load that He lays upon me?" There was no answering such reasoning. Whatever might have been the claim of Jesus upon others, He clearly had an indisputable right to the loyal obedience of one whom He had made perfectly whole.

Follow me briefly in this. If you have been saved by the grace of God, your salvation has put you under obligation henceforth to do what Jesus bids you. Are you redeemed? Then you are not your own; you are bought with a price. Have you been in consequence of what the Lord has done for you rescued from Satanic slavery and adopted into the divine family? It clearly follows that because you are sons, you should be obedient to the law of the household; for is not this a first element of sonship, that you should reverence the great Father of the family? The Lord has been pleased to put away your sin; you are forgiven, but does not pardon demand amendment? Shall we go back to the old sins from which we have been cleansed? Shall we live in the iniquities from which we have been washed by the blood of our Lord Jesus? That is horrible to think of. It would be nothing less than devilish for a man to say, "I have been forgiven, and therefore I will sin again." There is no remission where there is no repentance. The guilt of sin remains on that man in whom the love of sin still remains. Let us practically feel the force of this and henceforth follow after purity and righteousness.

If Christ has wrought His great work in you, you have experienced the love of God and, therefore, if God has so loved you, you are bound to love Him in return. If God has so loved you, must you not also love your brother man? Do not love for God and love for man spring up as a sure consequence of the love of God shed abroad in the heart? Does not everyone see the necessity that calls for the one love to follow the other? But love is the mother of obedience: thus everything connected with our Lord lays us under obligation to obey Him. There is not a single blessing of the covenant but what necessarily entails its corresponding duty. And here I scarcely like to say *duty*, for these blessings of the covenant make duty to be our privilege and holiness to be our delight. Henceforth redeemed from sin, we would live no longer therein. Henceforth made heirs of heaven, we endeavor to lead the heavenly life so that even while we are below, our conversation may be in heaven, from which we look for the Savior, the Lord Jesus Christ.

Brethren, He that made you whole has commanded this and that to be done by you. I counsel you to keep the King's commandment. As Mary said to the waiters at the wedding at Cana, so say I to you: "Whatsoever he saith unto you, do it" (John 2:5). Does He bid you pray, then pray without ceasing. Does He bid you watch as well as pray, then guard every act and thought and word. Does He bid you love your brethren? Then love them fervently with a pure heart. Does He bid you serve them and humble your-self for His sake? Then do so and become the servant of all. Has He said, "Be ye holy; for I am holy" (1 Pet. 1:16)? Then aim at this by His Holy Spirit. Has He said, "Be ye therefore perfect, even as your Father which is in heaven is perfect" (Matt. 5:48)? Then strive after perfection, for He who made you whole has a right to direct your way, and it will be both your safety and your happiness to submit yourself to His commands.

The Sense of Constraint

"He that made me whole, the same said unto me, take up thy bed and walk." He made him whole by saying, "Rise, take up thy bed." The carrying of the bed was part and parcel of the cure. The first part of the healing word was "Rise," but the second was "take up thy bed." It was not an ordinary word that Jesus spoke to that man—a mere word of advice, warning, or command—it was a word full of power, like that which created light out of darkness. When the Lord said to the poor man, "Rise," the man did rise. A thrill went through him. Those stagnant blood vessels felt the lifeblood stir and flow, those dormant nerves were aroused to sensations of health, those withered sinews and muscles braced themselves for energetic action, for omnipotence had visited the impotent man and restored him.

It must have been a wondrous joy to the long enervated, nerve-less, powerless frame to be capable of healthy motion, to be equal to bearing a happy burden. The joyful man rolled up his bed, threw it on his back, and marched abroad with the best of them. The bed carrying was part of the cure and proof of the cure. The paralytic man had not been called upon to deliberate as to whether he should rise or not, but Jesus said, "Rise," and the man stood upright. The same Word said, "take up thy bed," the bed was up at once, and according to the last word "walk," the man walked with delight. It was all done by the power of the one thrilling sentence that waited not to be questioned but accomplished the end for which the Lord had sent it.

Not unwillingly did the restored man carry his bed, yet he did it of constraint, for the same power that made him whole made him obedient. Before the divine energy had touched him, he seemed scarcely to have any will at all, and the Lord had to hunt to find a will in him, saying, "Wilt thou be made whole?" But now he cheerfully wills obedience to his benefactor and, in the force of the command, he carried out the Lord's word. I say that his taking up his bed and walking was done by Christ's enabling and by Christ's constraining, and I pray that you may know by experience what this means. What I want you to feel is this: "I cannot help obeying Christ, for by His Holy Spirit He has spoken me into a life that will never die and never be vanquished. He has spoken a word in me that has a continuous force over me and thrills me through and through continually. I can no more help seeking to obey Christ than this man could help carrying his bed when the Lord, by a word of power, had bid him do so."

Look at this, and be instructed and warned. Do you feel reluctant to enter upon your Lord's service because you are conscious of weakness? Has the devil tempted you to draw back from obedience because of your unfitness? Do you hesitate? Do you tremble? Surely you need to draw near to the Lord again and hear His voice anew. Take your Bible and let Him speak to you again out of the Word, and may the same thrill that awoke you out of your death sleep wake you out of your lethargy. There is need that the living Word of God should come home to your inmost soul again with that same miraculous power that dwelt in it at first. "Quicken me, O Lord," (Ps. 119:107) is David's prayer, but it suits me every day, and I think the most of God's people would do well to use it daily. "Lord, speak life in me now as You did at first. Speak power, speak spiritual force into me."

"The love of Christ constraineth us," says the apostle (2 Cor. 5:14): this constraint is what we want to feel more and more. We need divine life perpetually to carry us forward to acts of obedience. We do not want to destroy willinghood, but we would have it quickened into entire subservience to the will of the Lord. Like Noah's ark on dry land, the will keeps its place by its own dead weight. Oh, for a flood of grace to move, to lift, to upbear it, and to carry it away by a mighty current. We would be borne before the love of Christ as a tiny piece of wood is drifted by the gulf stream or as one of the specks that dance in the sunbeam would be carried by a rushing wind. As the impulse that began with Jesus found the poor man passive because utterly unable to be otherwise and then impelled him on to active movements as with a rush of power, so may it ever be with us throughout life. May we forever yield to the divine impulse.

To be passive in the Lord's hands is a good desire, but to be what I would call actively passive, to be cheerfully submissive, willingly to give up our will, this is a higher spiritual mood. We must live, and yet not we, but Christ in us. We must act, and yet we must say, He that made me whole bade me do this holy deed, and I do it because His power moves me. If I have done well, I lay the honor at His feet. If I hope to do well in the future, it is because I hope for strength from Him to do well, believing that He will work in me by that same power that converted me at the first. Endeavor to abide under this influence. May the Holy Spirit bring you there!

My last word is a practical lesson. The Church of God on earth at this present time anxiously desires to spread her influence over the world. For Christ's sake we wish to have the truths we preach acknowledged and the precepts that we deliver obeyed. But mark, no church will ever have power over the masses of this or any other land except in proportion as she does them good. The day has long since passed in which any church may hope to prevail on the plea of history. "Look at what we were," is a vain appeal: men only care for what we are. The church that glorifies itself with the faded laurels of past centuries and is content to be inactive today is near to its inglorious end.

In the race of usefulness, men nowadays care less about the pedigree of the horse and more about the rate at which it can run. The history of a congregation is of small account compared with the practical good that it is doing. If any church under heaven can show that it is making men honest, self-controlled, pure, moral, holy, that it is seeking out the ignorant and instructing them, that it is seeking out the fallen and reclaiming them, that in fact it is turning moral wastes into gardens and taking the weeds and briars of the wilderness and transforming them into precious fruit-bearing trees, the world will be ready to hear its claims and consider them. If a church cannot prove its usefulness, the source of its moral strength will have gone. Indeed, something worse than this will have happened, for its spiritual strength will have gone, too, for a barren church is manifestly without the fruitful Spirit of God.

You may, if you will, dignify your minister by the name of bishop. You may give to your deacons and elders grand official titles, you may call your place of worship a cathedral, you may worship if you will with all the grandeur of pompous ceremonial and the adornments of music and incense and the like, but you shall have only the semblance of power over human minds unless you have something more than these. But if you have a church, no matter by what name it is called, that is devout, that is holy, that is living unto God, that does good in its neighborhood, that by the lives of its members spreads holiness and righteousness, if you have a church that is really making the world whole in the name of Jesus, you shall in the long run find that even the most carnal and thoughtless will say, "The church that is doing this good is worthy of respect, therefore let us hear what it has to say."

Living usefulness will not screen us from persecution, but it will save us from contempt. A holy church goes with authority to the world in the name of Jesus Christ its Lord, and this force the Holy Spirit uses to bring human hearts into subjection to the truth. Oh, that the Church of God would believe in Jesus' power to heal sick souls. Recollect this man, thirty-eight years sick, had been longer ill than Christ had lived on earth. He had been seven years afflicted before Christ was born. Even so, this poor world has been long afflicted. Years before the Pentecost or the birth of the present visible Church, the poor sinful world lay at the pool and could not stir. We must not be hopeless about it, for yet the Lord will cast sin out of it. Let us go in Jesus Christ's name and proclaim the everlasting gospel, and say, "Rise, take up thy bed, and walk," and it shall be done, and God shall be glorified and we shall be blessed.

The miracle seems to me to teach that the power of Christ to save from sin does not lie in the person saved, it lies wholly in Jesus Himself. Further, I learn that though the person to be saved is so far gone that you could scarcely expect faith of him, yet the gospel coming to him can bring faith with itself and do its own work from the very beginning. What if I say that the gospel is a seed that makes its own soil! It is a spark that carries its own fuel with it. It is a life that can implant itself within the ribs of death, ay, between the jaws of destruction. The Eternal Spirit comes with His own light and life and creates men in Christ Jesus to the praise of the glory of His grace. Oh, the marvel of this miracle! I was never led more greatly to admire the splendor of the power of Christ to rescue men from sin than at this time.

Chapter Two

An Astounding Miracle

And they went into Capernaum; and straightway on the sabbath day he entered into the synagogue, and taught. And they were astonished at his doctrine: for he taught them as one that had authority, and not as the scribes. And there was in their synagogue a man with an unclean spirit; and he cried out, Saying, Let us alone; what have we to do with thee, thou Jesus of Nazareth? art thou come to destroy us? I know thee who thou art, the Holy One of God. And Jesus rebuked him, saying, Hold thy peace, and come out of him. And when the unclean spirit had torn him, and cried with a loud voice, he came out of him. And they were all amazed, insomuch that they questioned among themselves, saying, What thing is this? what new doctrine is this? for with authority commandeth he even the unclean spirits, and they do obey him. And immediately his fame spread abroad throughout all the region round about Galilee—Mark 1:21–28.

YOU WILL FIND THE SAME narrative in Luke 4:31–37. It will be handy for you to be able to refer to this second passage, from which I shall quote one or two matters.

These two evangelists commence their narrative by telling us of the singular authority and power that accompanied the Savior's teaching—authority, so that no man dare question His doctrine;

power, so that every man felt the force of the truth that He delivered. "They were astonished at his doctrine: for his word was with power" (Luke 4:32). Why was it that the Savior's teaching had such a remarkable power about it? Was it not, first, because He preached the truth? There is no power in falsehood except so far as men choose to yield to it because it flatters them. But there is great force in truth, and the truth makes its own way into the soul. As long as men have consciences, they cannot help feeling when the truth is brought to bear upon them. Even though they grow angry, their very resistance proves that they recognize the force of what is spoken.

Moreover, the Savior spoke the truth in a very natural, sincere manner: the truth was in Him, and it flowed freely from Him. His manner was truthful as well as His content. There is a way of speaking truth so as to make it sound like a lie. Perhaps there is not greater injury done to truth than when it is spoken in a doubtful manner, with none of the accent and emphasis of conviction. Our Savior spoke as the oracles of God. He spoke truth as truth should be spoken—without pretensions and naturally, as one who did not preach professionally but preached out of the fullness of His heart. We all know how sermons from the heart go to the heart.

Moreover, our great Exemplar delivered His teaching as one who most heartily believed what He was speaking, who spoke what He did know, yea, spoke of things that were His own. Jesus had no doubts, no hesitancy, no questions, and His style was as calmly forcible as His faith. Truth seemed to be reflected from His face just as it shone forth from God in all its native purity and splendor. He could not speak otherwise than He did, for He spoke as He was, as He felt, and as He knew. Our Lord spoke as one whose life supported all that He taught. Those who knew Him could not say, "He speaks one way, but He acts another." There was about His whole conduct and manners that which made Him the fit person to utter the truth, because the truth was incarnate and embodied and exemplified in His own person. Well might He speak with great assurance when He could say, "Which of you convinceth me of sin?" (John 8:46). He was Himself as pure as the truth that He proclaimed. He was not a speaking machine, sounding out something with which it has no vital connection; but out of the midst of His own heart flowed rivers of living waters. Truth overflowed at His lips from the deep well of His soul. It was in Jesus and therefore came from Him. What He poured forth was His own life, with which He was endeavoring to saturate the lives of others. Consequently, for all these reasons, and many besides, Jesus spoke as one who had authority: His tone was commanding; His teaching was convincing.

Meanwhile, the Holy Spirit, who had descended upon Jesus in His baptism, rested upon Him and bore witness by His divine operations in the consciences and hearts of men (John 16:7–11). If Jesus spoke of sin, the Spirit was there to convince the world of sin. If He set forth a glorious righteousness, the Holy Ghost was there to convince the world of righteousness. When He told men of the coming judgment, the Holy Spirit was present to make them know that a judgment would surely come at which each of them must appear. Because of His unlimited anointing by the Spirit, our Lord spoke with power and authority of the most astonishing kind, so that all who heard Him were compelled to feel that no ordinary rabbi stood before them.

That power and that authority were seen all the more in contrast with the scribes, who spoke hesitatingly and quoted authority. The scribes begged permission to venture an opinion, supporting their ideas by the opinion of this rabbi, although it was questioned by another rabbi. They spent their time in tying and untying knots before the people, quibbling about matters that had no practical importance whatever. They were wonderfully clear upon the tithing of mint and anise, copiously enlarged upon the washing of cups and basins, and were profound upon phylacteries and borders of garments. They were at home with such matters that would neither save a soul nor slay a sin nor suggest a virtue. While handling the Scriptures, they were mere word triflers, letter men, whose primary purpose was to show their own wisdom. Such attempts at oratory and word spinning were as far as the poles asunder from the teachings of our Lord. Self-display never entered into the mind of Jesus. He was so absorbed in what He had to teach that His hearers did not exclaim, "What a preacher he is!" but exclaimed, "What a word this is!" and "What new teaching this is!" The word and the teaching brought their admirable authority and amazing power to subdue men's minds and hearts by the energy of truth. Men acknowledged that the Great Teacher had taught them something worth knowing and had so impressed it upon them that there was no shaking themselves free of it.

When they were beginning to perceive this authority in His

Word, our Lord determined to prove to them that there was real power at the back of His teaching, that He had a right to use such authority, for He was Jesus Christ, the Son of God, clothed with divine authority and power. It occurred to Him to display before their eyes the fact that as there was power about His speech, there was also power about Himself, that He was mighty in deed as well as in word. Consequently, He wrought the miracle now before us. This most astounding deed of authority and power has been passed over by certain expositors as having too little of incident about it to be of much interest, whereas to my mind, it rises in some respects above all other miracles and is certainly excelled by no other miracle in its forcible demonstration of our Lord's authority and power. It is the first miracle that Mark mentions. It is the first that Luke gives us. And it is in some respects the first of miracles, as I hope I may show before I have finished.

Remember, however, that the object of the miracles is to reveal more fully the power and authority of our Lord's Word and to let us see by signs following that His teaching has an omnipotent force about it. This truth is much needed at the present moment, for if the gospel does not still save men, if it is not still "the power of God unto salvation to every one that believeth" (Rom. 1:16), then the attacks of skepticism are not easily repelled. But if the gospel is still a thing of power over the minds of men, a power conquering sin and Satan, let them say what they like; our only answer shall be to lament their doubts and to scorn their scorning. Oh, for an hour of the Son of man! Oh, where is He that trod the sea and bade the rage of hell subside with a word?

Our Lord Selects a Most Needy Person on Whom to Prove His Power

This person was, first, *one possessed*. A devil dwelt within him. We cannot explain this fact any more than we can explain mental illness. Many things that happen in the world of the mind are quite inexplicable and, for that matter, so are many facts in the world of matter. We accept the recorded fact—an evil spirit entered into this man and dwelt in him. Satan, you see, is always trying to imitate God, to caricature Him; so when God became incarnate, it occurred to Satan to become incarnate, too. And this man I may call, without any misuse of words, an incarnate devil; or at any rate, the devil was incarnated in him. The man had become like a devil in human form and so was in a certain manner the opposite of our Lord Jesus. In Jesus dwelt the fullness of the Godhead bodily by an eternal union; in this man the devil dwelt for a while. Is this not an awful picture? But note the fact, the man through whom Jesus selects to prove His power and authority was so far gone that the foul fiend controlled his mind and made a kennel of his body.

I wonder whether a person of whom this man is the emblem would come into our congregation today, for I have seen such people. I have not dared personally to apply such an epithet to any man, but I have heard it applied. I have heard disgusted friends and indignant neighbors, worn out with the drunken profanity or horrible filthiness of some man, say, "He does not seem to be a man; he acts like the evil one." Or when it has been a woman, they have said, "All that is womanly is gone; she seems to be a female fiend." If such a person were to read this sermon, let him or her take note that there is help, hope, and health even for that person. The power of Jesus knows no limit. Upon one who was the devil's own did our gracious Lord display His authority and power in connection with His gospel teaching. And He is not less able now than then.

This man, further, *was one whose personality was to a great extent merged in the evil one.* Read the twenty-third verse: "There was in their synagogue a man with an unclean spirit." The rendering might be equally accurate if we read it, "A man in an unclean spirit." Do you see that? Not only a man with an unclean spirit in him but also a man in an unclean spirit. The phrase is like when we speak of a man being in drink. For liquor to be in a man does not mean half as much as for a man to be in liquor. To give a more pleasant illustration, we speak of a man as being "in love"; he is absorbed in his affection. We do not express a tenth as much if we say that love is in the man.

A man can be in a rage, in a passion, and even so was this man in an evil spirit. He was completely ruled by the evil one. The poor person had no power over himself whatever and was not himself actually responsible. As far as the narrative is concerned, the man himself hardly appears. It is the unclean spirit that cries out, "Let us alone; I know thee who thou art." These are words spoken by the man, but they are the sentiments of the demon who used the man's organs of speech according to his own will. The man was hardly a man with a will or wish of his own; in fact, you do not notice him till you see him flung down into the midst of the syna-gogue. You see the real man only when the Savior raises him up before them all unharmed and rational. Until the miracle is wrought, the man is lost in the unclean spirit that dominates him.

Have you never seen such people? You say sometimes, and you say truly, "Alas, poor wretch! The drink has the mastery over him. He would never do such things if he were not drunk." We do not mean to excuse him by such an expression; far from it. Or it may be the person is a gambler, and you say, "He is addicted to gambling. Though he impoverishes his wife and children, yet he is possessed by that spirit so completely that he has not the mind nor the will to resist the temptation." Or it may be that person is carried away with unchaste affections, and we say, "How sad! There was something about the man that we used to like. In many points he was admirable, but he is so deluded by his bad passions that he does not seem to be himself." We almost forget the man and think mainly of the dreadful spirit that has degraded him below the beasts. It was this type of person that our Lord selected as the plat-form whereon to show His power. Jesus Christ is able to deliver such as are led captive at the will of Satan. Though they seem wholly given up and utterly abandoned to the dominion of a terrible sin, yet Jesus can break off the iron yoke from their neck and bring them into the liberty of holiness.

Note further, it was a man *in whom the evil spirit was at his worst.* Kindly look at Luke 4:33, and you will see that in this man there was "a spirit of an unclean devil." Think of that. The devil is never particularly clean at any time; what must an "unclean devil" be? The ruling spirit in the man was not only a devil but also an *unclean* devil. Satan sometimes cleans himself up and comes out quite bright and shining, like an angel of light, but do not mistake him. He is still a devil, for all his pretended purity. There are glittering sins and respectable sins, and these will ruin souls. But this poor man had a disreputable demon in him, a spirit of the foulest, coars-est, and most abominable order. I suppose this foul spirit would incite its victim to filthy talk and obscene acts. The evil one delights in sins against the seventh commandment. If he can lead men and women to defile their bodies, he takes special delight in such crimes. I doubt not that this poor creature was reduced to the most brutal form of animalism. I can well believe that his body was filthy and that in his talk—in all the thoughts that hurried through his poor brain and in all his actions—he went to a pitch of uncleanness upon which we need not imagine.

If we were to say of such a character as this man pictures, "Let us turn out of the way," who could blame us? We do not desire to go near to Satan in any shape, but most of all we would shun him when he is openly and avowedly unclean. You say, "We could not bear to hear the man speak; the very look of him is offensive"; nor is it strange that you should. There are women so fallen that modesty trembles to be seen in their company; and the feeling that makes you shudder at them is not to be condemned, so long as it does not spring from self-righteousness or lead to contempt. Yet, now, see it and wonder, our blessed Lord and Master fixed His eye of old on the man with the unclean devil. And today He fixes His eye of mercy on the basest and vilest of mankind, that in their conversion He may show the power and authority of His Word. Lord, do so at this moment. Let us see today the miracles of Your grace. Bring the chief of sinners to repentance! Raise up those who are fallen to the lowest degree!

In this man there did not seem to be anything for the Lord to begin upon. When you are trying to bring a man to the Savior, you study him to see where you can touch him, what there is in him that you can work upon. Perhaps he is a good husband though he is a drunkard, and you wisely attempt to work upon his family affections. If a man has some point of character upon which you can rest your lever, your work is comparatively easy. But with some people, you examine them from top to bottom and cannot find a spot for hope to rest upon. They seem so utterly gone that there is neither reason nor conscience nor will nor power of thought left in them. Of all this the possessed man in the synagogue is a striking emblem, for when the Lord comes into the synagogue, the poor wretch does not begin to pray, "Lord, heal me." No, his first cry is, "Let us alone." He does not seem to resist this cry of the evil spirit in him, though it was so much to his own injury, but he goes on to say, "What have we to do with thee, thou Jesus of Nazareth? Art thou come to destroy us? I know thee who thou art."

The possessed man seems wholly lost in the dominating spirit of evil that permeates his entire being. I do not care how far a man has gone in outward sin, if he has some point left in him of common honesty or love to his family or good-heartedness, you know where to commence operations, and your work is hopeful. Even leviathan has some crevice between his scales, though they be shut up together as with a closed seal. There is some joint in the harness of most men, even though a coat of armor may cover them from head to foot. But of those outcasts of whom I am now writing, there is neither foothold for hope or for faith nor more than a bare ledge for love. As the man in the synagogue was shut up within the demon's influence, so are some men encompassed by their iniquity, blocked up by their depravity. Yet the great Upraiser of the fallen can rescue even these. He is able to save unto the uttermost.

One other matter makes the case still more terrible: he was a man upon whom religious observances were lost. He was in the synagogue on the Sabbath, and I do not suppose that this was anything unusual. The worst man of all is one who can attend the means of grace and yet remain under the full power of evil. For those poor outside sinners who know nothing of the gospel and never go to the house of God there remains at least the hope that the very novelty of the Holy Word may strike them. But for those who are continually in our churches, what shall be done for them if they remain in sin? It is singular but true that Satan will come to a place of worship. He did it so long back as the days of Job, "when the sons of God came to present themselves before the LORD, and Satan came also among them" (Job 2:1).

The evil spirit led this unhappy man to the synagogue that morning, and it may be he did so with the idea of disturbing the teaching of the Lord Jesus Christ. I am glad he was there. I wish that all the slaves of sin and Satan would come to Sunday's worship. They are then within range of the gospel gun, and who can tell how many may be reached? Yet how sad it was that the influences of religious worship had altogether failed to rescue this man from his servitude! They sang in the synagogue, but they could not sing the evil spirit out of him. They read the lessons of the day in the synagogue, but they could not read the foul spirit out of him. They gave addresses from passages of Scripture, but they could not address the unclean spirit out of him. No doubt some of the godly prayed for him, but they could not pray the devil out of him. Nothing can cast out Satan but the word of Jesus Himself. His own word, from His own lip, has power and authority about it, but everything short of that falls to the ground. O divine Redeemer, let Your omnipotence be displayed in turning great sinners into sincere penitents!

You see, then, what a terrible case the Master selected. I have not exaggerated, I am sure. Oh, the comfort that lies in the thought that He still chooses to save persons, of whom this wretched being is the fit emblem and representative! There is hope for the vilest of the vile.

Our Lord Enounters a Firmly Entrenched Enemy

The evil spirit in this man had entrenched himself against the assault of Christ, for *he had the man fully at his command*, making him say and do whatever he pleased. He had that man so at his command that he brought him to the synagogue that day, and *he compelled him to become a disturber of the worship*. Quietness and order should be in the gatherings of God's people, but this poor soul was egged on to cry out and make horrible noises so as to raise great tumult in the congregation. The Jews allowed all the liberty they could to persons possessed, and so long as their behavior was bearable, these persons were tolerated in the synagogues. But this poor mortal broke through the bounds of propriety, and his cries were a terror to all. But see, the Lord Jesus deals with this disturber; this is the very man in whom He will be glorified. So have I seen my Lord convert His most furious enemy and enlist into His service the most violent of opposers.

The evil one compelled his victim to beg to be left alone: as we have it here: "Let us alone." In the Revised Version of Luke the same rendering is up in the margin, but in the text we have "Ah!" While the Lord Jesus was teaching, there was suddenly heard a terrible "Ah!" A horrible, hideous outcry startled all, and these words were heard: "Ah! What have we to do with thee?" It was not the voice of supplication, but was distinctly the reverse. It was a prayer not *for* mercy but *against* mercy. The translation is however quite good if we read, "Let us alone." Is it not a horrible thing when Satan leads men to say, "Do not trouble us with your gospel! Do not bother us with religion! Do not come here with your truth! Let us alone!" These men claim the wretched right to perish in their sins, the liberty to destroy their own souls. We know who rules when men speak like this: it is the prince of darkness who makes them hate the light. This cruel kindness we cannot grant them. How can we stand by and see them perish? Yet how sad the moral condition of one who does not wish to be made pure! You would think it impossible for Jesus to do anything with a man when he is crying out,

"Let us alone"; yet it was the evil spirit in this man that our Lord met and overcame. Is there not encouragement for us to deal with those who give us no welcome but shut the door in our faces?

The foul spirit *made the man renounce all interest in Christ;* he made him say, "What have we to do with thee, thou Jesus of Nazareth?" This was a disclaimer of all connection with the Savior. The spirit almost resented the Savior's presence as an intrusion. The voice seems to cry to Jesus, "I have nothing to do with you. Go your way and let me alone. I do not want you. Whatever you can do to save or bless me is hereby refused. Only let me alone." Now, when a man deliberately says, "I will have nothing to do with your Jesus, I want no pardon, no salvation, no heaven," I think that most of you would say, "That is a hopeless case. We had better go elsewhere." Yet even when Satan has led a man this length, the Lord can drive him out. He is mighty to save. He can change even the hardest heart.

The unclean spirit did more than that: *he caused this man to dread the Savior* and made him cry out, "Ah! Art thou come to destroy us?" Many persons are afraid of the gospel. To them religion wears a gloomy aspect. They do not care to hear of it for fear it should make them depressed and rob them of their pleasures. "Oh," say they, "religion would drive me mad." Thus Satan by his detestable falsehoods makes men dread their best friend and tremble at that which would make them happy forever.

A further entrenchment Satan had cast upon: *he made his victim yield an outward assent to the gospel.* "I know thee who thou art," said the spirit, speaking with the man's lips, "the Holy One of God." Of all forms of Satan's devices, this is one of the worst for workers, when men say, "Yes, yes, what you say is very correct!" You talk with them about Jesus, and they answer, "Yes, sir. It is quite true. I am much obliged to you, sir." You preach the gospel, and they say, "He made an interesting message and he is a very clever man!" You buttonhole them and speak about the Savior, and they reply, "It is very kind of you to talk to me so earnestly. I always admire this sort of thing. Zeal is much to be commended in these days." This is one of the strongest of earthworks, for the cannonballs sink into it, and their force is gone. This makes Satan secure in his hold on the heart. Yet the Savior dislodged this demon and therein displayed His power and authority.

Have I not proved my point? Jesus selected a most unhappy

individual to become an instance of His supremacy over the powers of darkness. He selected a most firmly entrenched spirit to be chased out of the nature that had become his stronghold.

Our Lord Conquered in a Remarkable Manner

The conquest *began as soon as the Savior entered the synagogue* and was thus under the same roof with the devil. Then the evil one began to fear. That first cry of "Ah" or "Let us alone" shows that the evil spirit knew his Conqueror. Jesus had not said anything to the man. No, but the presence of Christ and His teaching are the terror of fiends. Wherever Jesus Christ comes in, Satan knows that he must leave. Jesus has come to destroy the works of the devil, and the evil one is aware of his fate. As soon as you go into a house with the desire to bring the inmates to Christ, it will be telegraphed to the bottomless pit directly. As insignificant as you may think of yourself, you are a very dangerous person to Satan's kingdom if you go in the name of Jesus and declare His gospel. The Lord Jesus Christ opened the book and read in the synagogue, and soon His explanation and His teaching with authority and power made all the evil spirits feel that their kingdom was shaken. "I beheld," said our Lord at another time, "Satan as lightning fall from heaven" (Luke 10:18), and that fall was commencing in this "beginning of the gospel of Jesus Christ, the Son of God" (Mark 1:1). The first token of our Lord's triumph was the evident alarm that caused the evil spirit to cry out.

The next sign was that *the devil began to offer terms to Christ*, for I take it that is the reason he said, "I know thee who thou art, the Holy One of God." He confronted our Lord not with the hostile doubt, "If thou be the Son of God," but with the complaisant compliment, "I know thee who thou art." "Yes," the false spirit said, "I will allow this man to declare his creed and acknowledge himself one of the orthodox, and then perhaps I shall be let alone. The man is sound in his views, and so my living in him cannot be a bad thing after all. I am quite willing to admit all the claims of Jesus, so long as He will not interfere with my rule over the man." The evil one had opened his Bible and knew that Daniel had called Jesus "The Most Holy," and so he calls Him "The Holy One of God." "I am quite willing to admit it all," says the devil, "only let me reside in the man. Do not meddle with me, and this man's lips shall confess the truth."

And so, when Jesus comes in His power and men hear His Word, this deceitful compromise is often proposed and attempted. The sinner says, "I believe it all. I deny nothing. But I mean to keep my sin, and I do not intend to feel the power of the gospel so as to repent and have my sin chased out of me. I will agree to the gospel, but I will not allow it to control my life." However, this coming to terms shows that the fallen spirit knows his Destroyer. He is willing to crouch, to cringe, to fawn, and even to bear testimony to the truth if he may but be allowed to keep in his den—that den a human soul. Liar as he is, it must go sadly against the grain for him to say, "I know thee who thou art"; yet he will do this if he may be allowed to keep dominion. So when Jesus draws near to men's minds, they say, "We will be orthodox, we will believe the Bible, and we will do anything else you prescribe, only do not disturb our consciences, interfere with our habits, or dislodge our selfishness." Men will accept anything rather than renounce their sin, their pride, their ease.

Then came our Lord's real work on this man: *He gave the evil spirit short and sharp orders.* "Silence! Come out!" Jesus rebuked him. The word implies that He spoke sharply to him. How else could He speak to one who was maliciously tormenting a man who had done him no harm? The Greek word might be read, "Be muzzled." It is a harsh word that is appropriate for an unclean, tormenting spirit: "Silence! Come out." That is exactly what Jesus means that the devil shall do when He delivers men from him. He says to him, "Come out of the man. I do not want spiritual talk and orthodox declarations. Hold your peace and come out of him." It is not for evil spirits nor yet for ungodly men to try to honor Christ by their words. Traitors bring no honor to those they praise. Liars cannot bear witness to the truth or, if they do, they damage its cause.

"Be still," says Jesus, and then, "Come out." He speaks as a man might call a dog out of a kennel: "Come out." "Oh," says the unclean spirit, "let me stay, and the man shall go to church; he shall even go to the sacrament." "No," says the Lord. "Come out of him. You have no right within him. He is Mine, and not yours. Come out of him!" The Master calls at this moment and says to the sin in a man, "Come out of him! Sin must stop in you or it will ruin you forever. Are you not eager to be rid of it?"

Now see the conquest of Christ over the unclean spirit. *The fiend did not dare to utter another word,* though he went as near it as he could. He "cried with a loud voice." He made an inarticulate howling as he left the man. As he came out, he tried to do his victim some further injury, but in that also he failed. He tore at him and threw him down in the midst of the synagogue, but Luke adds, "He came out of him, and hurt him not" (Luke 4:35). From the moment when Jesus bade him, "Come out," his power to harm was gone; he came out like a whipped cur. See how Jesus triumphs. As He did this literally in the man in the synagogue, so He does it spiritually in thousands of cases.

The last act of the fiend was malicious but fruitless. I have seen a poor creature rolled in the dust of despair by the departing enemy, but he has soon risen to joy and peace. Have you not seen him bowed in repentance, weeping in the dismay of his spirit? But that has caused him no real harm; it has even been a benefit to him by causing him to feel a deeper sense of sin and driving him quite out of himself to the Savior. Oh, what a splendid triumph this is for our Lord when out of a great sinner the reigning power of sin is expelled by a word! How our Master tramples on the lion and the adder! How He treads under His feet the young lion and the dragon! If the Lord will speak with power today to any soul, however vicious or depraved or drunken, his reigning sins shall come out of him, and the poor sinner shall become a trophy of His sovereign grace.

The Savior Raises a Great Wonderment

The people that saw this were more astonished than they generally were at the Savior's miracles, for they said, "What thing is this? what new doctrine is this? for with authority commandeth he even the unclean spirits, and they do obey him." The wonder lay in this: here was *man at his very lowest*. He could not be worse—utterly and entirely possessed of Satan and carried away to an extreme degree by the force of evil. Now, under the preaching of the gospel the worst man who lives may be saved. While he is listening to the gospel, a power goes with it that can touch the hardest heart, subdue the proudest will, change the most perverted affections, and bring the most unwilling spirit to the feet of Jesus. I speak now what I do know, because I have seen it in hundreds of cases, that the least likely persons, about whom there seemed to be nothing whatever helpful to the work of grace or preparatory for it, have nevertheless been turned from the power of Satan to God. Such have been struck down by the preaching of the gospel, and the devil has been made to come out of them, there and then, and they have become new creatures in Christ Jesus. This creates a great wonderment and causes great staggering among the ungodly. They cannot understand it, but they ask, "What thing is this? and what new doctrine is this?" This is a convincing sign that makes the most unyielding unbeliever question his unbelief.

Notice, in this case, that *Jesus worked entirely and altogether alone.* In most of His other miracles He required faith. For salvation to come, there must be faith. But this miracle before us is a parable not so much of man's experience as of Christ's working, and that working is not dependent upon anything in man. When a man is commanded to stretch out his withered hand or told to go to the Pool of Siloam and wash, he does something, but in this case, the man is ignored. If he does anything, it is rather to resist than to assist. The devil makes him cry, "Let us alone; what have we to do with thee?" The Lord Jesus Christ here displays His sovereignty, His power, and His authority, utterly ignoring the man—consulting neither his will nor his faith—but sovereignly bidding the fiend, "Be silent and come out." The thing is done, and the man is delivered from his bondage before he has even had time to seek or pray.

The miracle seems to me to teach that the power of Christ to save from sin does not lie in the person saved, it lies wholly in Jesus Himself. Further, I learn that though the person to be saved is so far gone that you could scarcely expect faith of him, yet the gospel coming to him can bring faith with itself and do its own work from the very beginning. What if I say that the gospel is a seed that makes its own soil! It is a spark that carries its own fuel with it. It is a life that can implant itself within the ribs of death, ay, between the jaws of destruction. The Eternal Spirit comes with His own light and life and creates men in Christ Jesus to the praise of the glory of His grace. Oh, the marvel of this miracle! I was never led more greatly to admire the splendor of the power of Christ to rescue men from sin than at this time.

To conclude, I notice our Lord *did nothing but speak.* In other cases, He laid His hand upon the diseased or led them out of the city or touched them or applied clay or used spittle. But in this case, He uses only the instrumentality of His Word. He says, "Hold thy peace, and come out of him"; and the unclean spirit is evicted. The word of the Lord has shaken the kingdom of darkness and loosed the bonds of the oppressed. As when the Lord scattered the primeval darkness by the fiat, "Light be," so did Jesus give the word, and its own intrinsic power banished the messenger of darkness.

You who preach Christ, preach Him boldly! No coward lips must proclaim His invincible gospel! You who preach Christ, never choose your place of labor; never turn your back on the worst of mankind! If the Lord should send you to the borders of perdition, go there and preach Him with full assurance that it shall not be in vain. You who would win souls, have no preference as to which they shall be, or if you have a choice, select the very worst! Remember, my Master's gospel is not merely for the moralist in his respectable dwelling but is for the abandoned and fallen in the filthy dens of the outcast. The all-conquering light of the Sun of Righteousness is not for the dim dawn alone, to brighten it into the full blaze of day, but is meant for the blackest midnight that ever made a soul to shiver in the shadow of death. The name of Jesus is high over all—in heaven and earth and sky—therefore let us preach it with authority and confidence. Christ has said He will be with us, and therefore nothing is impossible. The Word of the Lord Jesus cannot fall to the ground; the gates of hell cannot prevail against it. The pleasure of the Lord shall prosper in His hand. The Lord shall bruise Satan under our feet shortly (Rom. 16:20).

I have gone to great lengths in this chapter because I desire to see sinners reached who have gone to great lengths. Oh, that they would accept this message of amazing mercy! He who has come to save sinners is God, and this is the surest ground of hope for the very worst. It is the Lord your God who speaks, "Look unto me, and be ye saved, all the ends of the earth: for I am God, and there is none else" (Isa. 45:22).

If our religion does no more in the world than any other, well then, despise it. If men can receive the gospel of Christ and yet live as they did before and be none the better for it, then tell us at once, that we may be undeceived, for our gospel is not wanted. But we bring you forward proofs. In our church there are scores and hundreds who are the proofs of what the living gospel can do. Many and many a story could I tell of a man who was a fiend in human shape, a man who, when he came home from work made it an hour of peril, for his wife and children fled to hide from him. But that man now, see him when he goes home, how he is welcomed by his wife, how the children run to meet him. You shall hear him sing more loudly now than ever he cursed before, and he who was once a ringleader in the army of Satan has now become a ringleader in the army of Christ. The Lord's is the glory of it. That is the argument: "Whereas I was blind, now I see."

Chapter Three

Simple But Sound

One thing I know, that, whereas I was blind, now I see.
—John 9:25.

DID YOU EVER READ this account of Jesus' healing the blind man and consider how wonderfully calm and collected our Lord must have been at this time? He had been preaching in the temple, talking to a multitude of Jews. The people grew furious with Him, and noticing a number of stones lying about on the floor that were used in repairing the temple, they took up these stones to cast at Him. He, by some means, forced a passage and escaped out of the midst of them. And when He came to the gate of the temple with His disciples—who seem to have followed Him in the lane that He was able to make through the throng of His foes—He saw this blind man. As if there had been no bloodthirsty foes at His heels, Jesus stopped—stopped as calmly as if an attentive audience had been waiting upon His lips—to look at the blind man.

The disciples stopped, too, but they paused to ask questions. How like ourselves! We are always ready to talk. How unlike the Master! He was always ready to act. The disciples wanted to know how the man came to be blind, but the Master meant to deliver the man from his blindness. We are very apt to be entering into speculative theories about the origin of sin or the cause of certain strange providences. But Christ is ever for seeking out not the cause but the remedy, not the reason for the disease but the way by which the disease can be cured.

The blind man is brought to Him. Christ asks him no questions. But spitting upon the dust, He stoops down and works the dust into mortar. When He has done this, taking it up in His hands, He applies it to what Bishop Hall calls the eyeholes of the man (for there were no eyes there) and plasters them up so that the spectators look on and see a man with clay upon his eyes. "Go," said Christ, "to the pool of Siloam, and wash." Some kind friends led the man, who was only too glad to go. Unlike Naaman, who made an objection to wash in the Jordan and be clean, the blind man was glad enough to avail himself of the divine remedy. He went, he washed the clay from his eyes, and he received his sight—a blessing he had never known before. With what rapture he gazed upon the trees! With what delight he lifted up his face to the blue sky! With what pleasure he beheld the costly, stately fabric of the temple! And afterward, with what pleasure he would look into the face of Jesus—the man who had given him his sight.

It is not my purpose to expound this miracle, but it clearly sets forth in sacred emblem the state of human nature. Man is blind. Father Adam put out our eyes. We cannot see spiritual things. We have not the spiritual picture; that has gone—gone forever. We are born blind. Christ comes into this world, and His gospel is despicable in men's esteem even as spittle—the thought of it disgusts most men. Gentility turns on its heel and says it will have nothing to do with it, and pomp and glory all say that it is a contemptible and base thing. Christ puts the gospel on the blind eye—a gospel that, like clay, seems as if it would make men more blind than before, but it is through "the foolishness of preaching" that Christ saves them that believe (1 Cor. 1:21). The Holy Spirit is like Siloam's pool. We go to Him, or rather He comes to us, and the convictions of sin produced by the gospel are washed away by the cleansing influences of the Divine Comforter. Then, behold, we, who were once so blind that we could see no beauty in divine things and no excellence in the crown jewels of God, begin to see things in a clear and heavenly light and rejoice exceedingly before the Lord.

But the blind man no sooner sees than he is brought before adversaries, and our text is a part of his testimony in defense of the "prophet" who had wrought the miracle upon him and who he did not as yet understand to be the Messiah.

"One thing I know, that, whereas I was blind, now I see." Although the parable furnishes an admirable topic, I prefer to keep to this verse and linger upon the various reflections it suggests.

An Unanswerable Argument

Every now and then, you and I are called into a debate regarding faith. People do not take things for granted, and it is proper that they should not. There have been ages in which any impostor could lead the public by the nose. Men would believe anything, and any crazy maniac who might stand up and pretend to be the Messiah would be sure to have some followers.

I think this age, with all its faults, is not so credulous as that which has gone by. There is a great deal of questioning, and there is some questioning where there should not be any. Men who stand high in official positions and who ought long ago to have had their faith established or to have renounced their position have ventured to question the very things they have sworn to defend. There is questioning everywhere, but to my mind it seems that we need not be afraid. If the gospel of God is true, it can stand any amount of questioning. I am more afraid of the deadness and lethargy of the public mind about religion than any sort of inquiry or controversy about it. As silver tried in the furnace is purified seven times, so the Word of God. The more it is put into the furnace, the more it will be purified, and the more beauteously the pure ore of revelation will glitter in the sight of the faithful.

Never be afraid of a debate, but never go into it unless you are well armed. And if you do go into it, mind that you take with you the weapon I am giving you. Though you may be unarmed in every other respect, if you know how to wield this weapon, you may, through grace, come off more than a conqueror. The argument that this man used was this, "Whereas I was blind, now I see."

It is forcible because it is a *personal argument*. I heard a person, the other day, use a similar argument. I had been laughing at a certain system of medicine that I thought was foolish. The person in question said, "Well, I can't laugh at it." "Why?" I asked. "Because," said he, "it cured me." Of course, I had no further answer. If this person had really been cured by such-and-such a remedy, it was to him an unanswerable argument. And to me, could he produce many other cases, it would be one that I would not wish to answer. The fact is, the personality of the thing gives it power. People tell us that in the pulpit, the minister should always say, "we," as editors do in writing. But we should lose all our power if we did. The minister of God is to use the first person singular and constantly to say, "I bear eyewitness for God that in my case, such-and-such a thing has been true." I will not blush or stammer to say, "I bear my personal witness to the truth of Christ's gospel in my own case." Lifted up from sin, delivered from bondage, from doubt, from fear, from despair, from any agony intolerable—lifted up to joys unspeakable and into the service of my God—I bear my own testimony.

I believe that your force in the world will be mightily increased if you constantly make your witness for Christ a personal one. I daresay my neighbor over there can tell what grace has done for him. Yes; but to me, to my own soul, what grace has done for me will be more of an establishment to me for my faith than what Christ has done for him. And if I stand up and declare what God's grace has done for this or that brother, it may do very well, but if I can say, "I myself have proved it," here is an argument that drives in the nail—ay, and clinches it, too. I believe that if you would prevail when you have to argue, you must do so by bearing a personal testimony to the value of faith in your own case, for that which you despise yourself you can never persuade others to value. "I believed, therefore have I spoken," said the psalmist (Ps. 116:10). Martin Luther was a man of strong faith, and therefore he kindled faith in others. That man will never move the world who lets the world move him, but the man who stands firm and says, "I *know*, I *know*, I *know* such-and-such a thing because it is burned into my own inner consciousness"—such a man's very appearance becomes an argument to convince others.

Moreover, this man's argument was *an appeal to men's senses*, and hardly anything can be supposed more forcible than that. "I was blind," said he. "You saw that I was. Some of you noticed me at the gate of the temple. I *was* blind, now I see. You can all see that I can look at you. You perceive at once that I have eyes, or else I could not see you in the way I do." He appealed to their senses. The argument that our holy faith needs at the present moment is a new appeal to the senses of men. You will ask me, "What is that?" The holy living of Christians. The change that the gospel works in men must be the gospel's best argument against all opposers. When the gospel was first preached in the island of Jamaica, some of the plantation owners objected grievously to it. They thought it improper to teach the slaves, but a missionary said, "What has been the effect of your servant Jack hearing the gospel?" The planter replied, "Well, he was constantly drunk before, but he is sober now. I could not trust him; he was a great thief, but he is honest now. He swore like a trooper before, but now I hear nothing objectionable come from his mouth." "Well," said the missionary, "then I ask you whether a gospel that has made such a change as that in the man must not be of God. I challenge you to put your influence into its scale rather than to work against it."

It is a compelling argument when we can bring forward the harlot who has been made chaste, when we can also show the drunkard who has been made sober, or, better still, when we can bring the careless, thoughtless man who has been made sedate and steady. To bring forward the man who cared not for God, nor Christ, who has been made to worship God with his whole heart and has put his confidence in Jesus, we think we have then presented to the world an argument that they will not soon answer.

If our religion does no more in the world than any other, well then, despise it. If men can receive the gospel of Christ and yet live as they did before and be none the better for it, then tell us at once, that we may be undeceived, for our gospel is not wanted. But we bring you forward proofs. In our church there are scores and hundreds who are the proofs of what the living gospel can do. Many and many a story could I tell of a man who was a fiend in human shape, a man who, when he came home from work made it an hour of peril, for his wife and children fled to hide from him. But that man now, see him when he goes home, how he is welcomed by his wife, how the children run to meet him. You shall hear him sing more loudly now than ever he cursed before, and he who was once a ringleader in the army of Satan has now become a ringleader in the army of Christ. The Lord's is the glory of it. That is the argument: "Whereas I was blind, now I see."

Do we not know of some who, when they came to make their profession of faith before the church, said, "If anyone had told me three months ago that I should be here, I should have knocked him down. If any man had said I should make a profession of faith in Jesus, I should have called him all the names in the world." But yet grace has changed the man, and his whole life is different now. Those who hate the change cannot help observing it. They hate religion, they say; but if religion does such things as these, the more of it the better.

Now we want, in the dark lanes and alleys of London and in our great wide streets, too, where there are large shops and places of business, we want to give the groveling world this argument, against which there is no disputing, that whereas there were some men blind, now they see. Whereas they were sinful, now they are virtuous. Whereas they despised God, now they fear Him. We believe this is the best answer for an unbelieving age. What a deal of writing there has been lately about and against the clergyman, Dr. Colenso! I think we should be doing much better if, instead of running after this heathenish bishop, we should be running after poor sinners. Instead of writing books of argument and entering into discussions, we should keep on each, in our sphere, endeavoring to convert souls, imploring the Spirit of God to come down upon us and make us spiritual fathers in Israel. Then we may say to the devil, "Well, sir, you have stolen a bishop, you have robbed us of a leader or two, but by the help of God, we have razed your territories, we have stolen away whole bands. Here they are, tens of thousands of men and women who have been reclaimed from the paths of vice, rescued from the destroyer, and made servants of the Lord." These are your best arguments, for there are no arguments like them—living personal witnesses of what divine grace can do.

A Satisfactory Piece of Knowledge

"One thing I know, that, whereas I was blind, now I see."

A love of knowledge is not uncommon. The desire for knowledge is almost universal. The attainment of it, however, is rare. But if a man shall attain the knowledge of Christ, he may take a high degree in the gospel, a satisfactory degree, a degree that shall land him safe into heaven, put the palm branch in his hand and the eternal song in his mouth, which is more than any worldly degrees will ever do. "One thing I *know*." The skeptic will sometimes overwhelm you with his knowledge. Those of you who have read but little and whose business occupations take up so much of your time that you probably never will be very profound students are often in danger of being attacked by men who can use long words, who profess to have read very great books, and claim to be very learned in sciences, the names of which you have scarcely ever heard. Meet them, but be sure you meet them with a knowledge that is better than theirs. Don't attempt to meet them on their own ground; meet them with this knowledge. "Well," you can say, "I know that you understand more than I do. I may not be highly educated, but I have a something in here that answers all your arguments, whatever they may be. I do not know what geology says; I may not understand all about history; I may not comprehend all the strange things that are daily coming to light; but one thing I know—it is a matter of absolute consciousness to me—that I, who was once blind, have been made to see."

Then just state the difference that the gospel made in you. Say that once, when you looked at the Bible, it was a dull, dry book. Say that when you thought of prayer, it was a dreary piece of work. Say that now the Bible seems to you a honeycomb full of honey and that prayer is your vital breath. Say that once you tried to get away from God and could see no excellence in the divine character, but now you are striving and struggling to get nearer to God. Say that once you despised the cross of Christ and thought it a vain thing for you to trust in it, but now you love it and would sacrifice your all for it. And this undoubted change in your own consciousness, this supernatural work in your own innermost spirit, shall stand you in the stead of all the arguments that can be drawn from all the sciences. Your one thing shall overthrow their thousand things if you can say, "Whereas I was blind, now I see."

Says one, "I don't know how that can be." Suppose that some-one has just discovered electricity and I have had an electric shock. Now, twenty people come and say, "There is no such thing as electricity. We do not believe in it for a moment." And there is one gentleman who proves by Latin that there cannot be such a thing as electricity, and another proves it mathematically by demonstration, and twenty others prove it in their different ways. I should say, "Well, I cannot answer you in Latin, I cannot overthrow you in logic, I cannot contradict that syllogism of yours. But one thing I know—I have had a shock of it—that I *do* know." I take it that my personal consciousness of having experienced an electric shock will be a better answer than all their learned sayings. And so, if you have ever felt the Spirit of God come into contact with you (and that is something quite as much within the reach of our consciousness as even the shock of electricity), and if you can say of that, "One thing I know, that cannot be beaten out of me or hammered out of my own consciousness, that whereas I was blind, now I see." If you can say that, it will be quite sufficient reply to all that the skeptic may bring against you.

How often are you assailed not only by the skeptic but also by our very profound doctrinal brethren! I know some very great doctrinal friends who, because our experience may not match theirs, will sit down and say, "Ah, you don't know the power of vital godliness!" They will write very severe things against us and say that we don't know the great secret and don't understand the inner life. You never need trouble yourself about these braggarts. Let them talk on until they have finished. But if you do want to answer them, do it humbly by saying, "Well, you may be right, and I may be mistaken. But yet I think I can say, 'One thing I know, that whereas I was blind, now I see.'" And I have known them to sometimes go to the length of saying, if we don't hold all their points of doctrine and go the whole eighteen ounces to the pound as they do—if we are content with sixteen, and keep God's weights and God's measures—"Ah, those people cannot be truly converted Christians; they are not so high in doctrine as we are!" We can answer them with this, "One thing I know, that whereas I was blind, now I see."

You sometimes meet with older believers, very good people who think themselves to be very wise, and they will put you into their sieve. Some of our brethren always carry a sieve with them. If they meet a young brother, they will try to sift him, and they will often do it very unkindly, asking him knotty questions. I always compare this to a man's testing a newborn child's health by putting nuts into his mouth and, if he cannot crack them, saying, "He is not healthy." I have known very difficult questions asked about such things as the exact difference between justification and sanctification, or something of that sort. I advise you to get all that sort of knowledge you can; but putting all of it together, it is not nearly equal in value to this small bit of knowledge: "One thing I know, that whereas I was blind, now I see."

Many of the old Puritanic books have I studied and tried to enrich my mind with the far-sought lore of the writers of them, but I tell you there are times when I would give up everything I have ever learned if I could but say for a certainty, "One thing I know, that whereas I was blind, now I see." And even now, though I have no doubt about my own acceptance in Christ and my having been brought to see, yet, compared with this piece of knowledge, I do count all the excellency of human knowledge—and all the rest of divine knowledge, too—to be but dross and dung, for this is the one thing needful, the one soul-saving piece of knowledge: "One thing I know, that whereas I was blind, now I see."

My dear reader, do you see a beauty in Christ? Do you see a loveliness in the gospel? Do you perceive an excellence in God your Father? Can you read your title clear to mansions in the skies?

Once you could not do this. Once you were a stranger to these things and your soul was dark as the darkest night without a star, without a ray of knowledge or of comfort. But now you see. Seek after more knowledge; but still, if you cannot attain it and if you tremble because you cannot grow as you would, remember this is enough to know for all practical purposes: "One thing I know, that whereas I was blind, now I see."

A Model Confession of Faith

This blind man did not do as some would have done. When he found his eyes, he did not use them to go and hunt out a quiet corner so that he might hide himself in it. He came out boldly before his neighbors, and then before Christ's enemies, and said, "One thing I know, that, whereas I was blind, now I see." Some of you have grace in your heart but have not courage to confess it. You have not put on your uniform. You call yourselves members of the Church Militant, but you are not dressed in the true scarlet. You do not come forward and wear the Master's badge and openly fight under His banner. I think it is very unkind of you and very dishonoring to your Master. There are not many who speak for Him, and it is a shame that you should hold your tongue. If He has given you eyes, I am sure you ought to give Him your tongue. If He has taught you to see things in a new light, I am sure you ought not to be unwilling to confess Him before men. After so much kindness in the past, it is cruel ingratitude to be ashamed to confess Him. You do not know how much you would comfort the minister. Converts are our sheaves, and you who do not join the Church do, as it were, rob us of our reward. No doubt you will be gathered into God's storehouse, but then we do not know anything about that. We want to see you gathered into God's storehouse here; we want to hear you boldly say, "Whereas I was blind, now I see."

You cannot tell how much good you might do to others. Your example would move your neighbors; your confession would be valuable to saints and might be a help to sinners. Your taking the decisive step might lead others to take it. Your example might be just the last grain cast into the scale that leads others to decide for the Lord. I am ashamed of you who once were blind yet now see but do not like to say so. I pray you lay the matter to heart and before long come out and say, "Yes, I cannot withhold it any longer. Whereas I was once blind, now I see."

"Well," says one, "I have often thought of joining the Church, but I can't be perfect." Now this man did not say, "I was once imperfect, and now I am perfect." Oh, no! If you were perfect, we would not receive you into church fellowship, because we are all imperfect ourselves and should fall out with you if we did take you in. We don't want those who say they are perfect. Let them go to heaven; that is the place for perfect ones, not here.

"Well," says someone else, "I have not grown in religion as I should like to do. I am afraid I am not as saintly as I would desire to be." Strive after a high degree of holiness, but remember that a high degree of holiness is not necessary to a profession of your faith. You are to make a profession as soon as you have any holiness, and the high degree of it is to come afterward.

"Ah," says another, "but I could not say much!" Nobody asked you to say much. If you can say, "Whereas I was blind, now I see," that is all we want. If you can but let us know that there is a change in you, that you are a new person, that you see things in a different light, that what was once your joy is now your sorrow and what was once a sorrow to you is now your joy—if you can say, "All things have become new"; if you can say, "I feel a new life heaving within my bosom; there is a new light shining in my eyes. I go to God's house now in a different spirit. I read the Bible and engage in private prayer, after quite a different fashion. And I hope my life is different and my language is not what it used to be. I try to curb my temper. I do endeavor to provide things honest in the sight of all men. My nature is different. I could no more live in sin as I once did than a fish could live on dry land or a man could live in the depths of the sea"—this is what we want of you.

Suppose now a person were to get up in the church meeting and say, "Brethren, I come to unite with you. I know the Greek Testament. I have also read a good deal in Latin. I understand the Vulgate. I can now, if you desire, give you the first chapter of Mark in Greek or the second chapter of Exodus in Hebrew. I have also, from my youth up, given myself to the study of the natural and applied sciences. I think I am master of rhetoric, and I am able to reason logically." Suppose he went on then to say what he knew about business, what a skillful tradesman he had been, and after going through that should say, "I have a great deal of theological knowledge. I have read the Church Fathers. I have studied Augustine. I could talk about all the ponderous tomes that were written in the ancient times. I am acquainted with all the writers on the Reformation, and I have studied the Puritans through and through. I know the points of difference between the great Reformed teachers, and I know the distinction between Zwingli and Calvin."

I am sure that if a man were to say all that, before I put it to the vote whether he should be admitted to Church membership, I should say, "This dear brother has not any idea of what he came here for. He came here to make a confession that he was a living man in Christ Jesus, and he has been trying only to prove to us that he is an educated man. That is not what we want." And I should begin to put to him some pointed questions, something like this: "Did you ever feel yourself a sinner? Did you ever feel that Christ was a precious Savior, and are you putting your trust in Him?" But you might say, "Why, that's just what he asked poor Mary, the servant girl, when she was in the meeting five minutes ago!" All that learned lumber is good enough in its place. I do not depreciate it. I wish every believer were a scholar. I love to see you great servants in the Master's cause. But the whole of that put together is not worth a straw compared with this: "One thing I know, that, whereas I was blind, now I see."

This is all we ask of you. We ask you only whether you wish to join the Church, to be able to confess that you are a changed character, that you are a new person, that you are willing to be obedient to Christ and to His ordinances, and then we are only too glad to receive you into our midst. Come out, come out, I pray you, who are hiding among the trees of the wood, come forth. Whosoever is on the Lord's side, let him come forth. It is a day of blasphemy and rebuke. He that is not with Christ is against Him, and he that gathers not with Him scatters abroad (Matt. 12:30). Come forth, come forth, you who have any spark of love for God, or else this shall be your doom: "Curse ye Meroz,...curse ye bitterly the inhabitants thereof; because they came not to the help of the LORD against the mighty" (Judg. 5:23).

A Very Clear and Manifest Distinction

Perhaps you cannot say, "One thing I know, that, whereas I was blind, now I see." Solemnly, as in the sight of God, I write to you; lend me your eyes, and may these few words of truth sink into your hearts! *Are there not some of you who cannot even say, "I was blind"?* You do not know your own blindness. You have the conceit to imagine that you are as good as most people and that if you have some faults, yet certainly you are not irretrievably lost. You have no idea that you are depraved, utterly depraved, saturated through and through, and rotten at the core. If I were to describe you in Scriptural language and say, "Thou art the man," you would be shocked at me for giving you so bad a character. You are amiable, your outward behavior has always been decorous, you have been generous and benevolent and, therefore, you think there is no need for you to be born again—no necessity for you to repent of sin. You think that the gospel is very suitable for those who have gone into foul, open sin; but you are too good rather than too bad!

O my reader, you are stone blind, and the proof that you are so is that you do not know your blindness! A man who is born blind does not know what it is to lose sight. The bright beams of the sun never made glad his heart and, therefore, he does not know his misery. Such is your state. You do not understand what it is that you have lost or what it is that you need. I pray God to do for you what you cannot do for yourself—make you feel now, once for all, that you are blind. There is hope for the man who knows his blindness—there is some light in the man who says he is all darkness—there is some good thing in the man who says he is all foul. If you can say, "Vile and full of sin I am," God has begun a good work in you. If you know your sin so as to feel your utterly ruined, lost estate, God has begun a good work in you. He will put away your sin and save your soul. Alas, there are many who do not know that they are blind!

And yet I know, to my sorrow, there are many of you who know that you are blind but *you don't see yet.* To know your blindness is good, but it is not enough. It would be a dreadful thing for you to go from an awakened conscience on earth to a tormenting conscience in hell. There have been some who have begun to find out that they are lost here and then have discovered that they are lost hereafter as well. I pray you do not tarry long in this state. If God has convinced you of sin, I pray you do not linger. The Lord is waiting to save you now. The way of salvation is simply this: trust Christ, and you are saved. Just as you are, rely upon Him, and you are saved. With no other dependence, with no other shadow of a hope, sinner, venture on Him, venture wholly, venture now. I hear the wheels of the Judge's chariot behind you. He comes! He comes! He comes! Fly, sinner, fly! I see God's bow in His awful hand, and

He has drawn the arrow to its very head. Fly, sinner! Fly, while yet the wounds of Christ stand open! Hide yourself there as in the cleft of the Rock of Ages. You have not lease of your life, you cannot tell that you shall ever see another Sabbath day to spend in pleasure. No more warnings may ever ring in your ears. Perhaps you will never have even another weekday to spend in drunkenness and blasphemy.

Sinner, turn! "Turn ye, turn ye from your evil ways; for why will ye die?" (Ez. 33:11). One of the two it must be—turn or die. Believe in Christ or perish with a great destruction. "He, that being often reproved hardeneth his neck, shall suddenly be destroyed, and that without remedy" (Prov. 29:1). You who are aroused and convinced, I pray you to trust Christ and live. The whole matter is very simple: "Whereas I was blind, now I see." Do you see that Christ can save you? Do you believe that He will save you if you trust Him? Then trust Him, and you are saved. The moment you believe, you are saved, whether you feel the comfort of it or not. And the thought arising from the full belief that you are saved will yield you the comfort that you will never find elsewhere.

It is written, "He that believeth on him is not condemned" (John 3:18). Then I am not condemned. Perhaps I feel at this present moment no joy, but then the thought that I am not condemned will also make me feel joy by and by. Yet I must not build on my joy, I must not build on my feelings, but simply on this, that God has said, "He that believeth and is baptized shall be saved" (Mk. 16:16). I, believing in Christ, am saved. And that is true of you also. It is true of every man, woman, or child who has put trust in Christ. You are saved, your sin is blotted out, your iniquity is forgiven, you are a child of God, the Lord accepts you. If you have really trusted Christ, you are an heir of heaven. Go and sin no more; go and rejoice in pardoning love; and God bless you, for Jesus' sake!

It is clear that if it is done in faith, the simplest action of life may be sublimely great. The flash of the wave as it covers Peter's net may be as sublime before the Lord as the glory of the Red Sea billow when it returned in its strength. God who sees a world in a drop sees wonders in the smallest act of faith. Do not, I pray you, think that sublimity lies in masses, to be measured by a scale, so that a mile shall be sublime and an inch shall be absurd. We measure not moral and spiritual things by rods and chains. The common act of fishing at Christ's word links Peter with all the principalities and powers and forces that in all ages have known this as their only law: "He spake, and it was done; he commanded, and it stood fast" (Ps. 33:9). We, too, shall have fellowship with the sublime if we know how to be perfectly obedient to the word of the Lord.

Chapter Four

At Thy Word

And Simon answering said unto him, Master, we have toiled all the night, and have taken nothing: nevertheless at thy word I will let down the net—Luke 5:5.

HOW VERY MUCH MAY simple obedience partake of the sublime! Peter went to take up the net and let it down into the sea, and he said as naturally as possible, *"At thy word* I will let down the net." But he was appealing to one of the grandest principles that rule among intelligent beings and to the strongest force that sways the universe: "At thy word." Great God, it is "at thy word" that seraphs fly and cherubs bow! Your angels who excel in strength do Your commandments hearkening to the voice of Your word. "At thy word" space and time first came into existence, and everything else that is.

"At thy word"—here is the cause of causes, the beginning of the creation of God. "By the word of God the heavens were of old" (2 Pet. 3:5), and by that word was the present constitution of this round world settled as it stands. When the earth was formless and dark, Your voice, O Lord, was heard, saying, "Let there be light" (Gen. 1:3), and "at thy word" light leaped forth. "At thy word" day and night took up their places, and "at thy word" the waters were divided from the waters by the firmament of heaven. "At thy word" the dry land appeared, and the seas retired to their channels. "At thy word" the globe was mantled over with green, and vegetable life began. "At thy word" appeared the sun and moon and stars, "for signs, and for seasons, and for days, and years" (Gen. 1:14). "At thy word" the living creatures filled the sea and air and land, and man at last appeared. Of all this we are well assured, for by "faith we understand that the worlds were framed by the word of God" (Heb. 11:3). Living in conformity with the word of our Lord, we feel ourselves to be in order with all the forces of the universe, traveling on the main track of all real existence. Is not this a sublime condition, even though it is seen in the common deeds of our everyday life?

It is not in creation alone that the word of the Lord is supreme, but in providence, too, its majestic power is manifested, for the Lord upholds "all things by the word of his power" (Heb. 1:3). Snow and rain and stormy winds are all fulfilling His word. "His word runneth very swiftly" (Ps. 147:15). When frost binds up the life floods of the year, the Lord sends forth His word and melts them (Ps. 147:18). Nature abides and moves by the word of the Lord. So, too, all matters of fact and history are beneath the supreme Word. Jehovah stands at the center of all things, as Lord of all He abides at the saluting point, and all the events of the ages come marching by at His word bowing to His sovereign will.

"At thy word," O God, kingdoms rise and empires flourish. "At thy word" races of men become dominant and tread down their fellows. "At thy word" dynasties die, kingdoms crumble, mighty cities become a wilderness, and armies of men melt away like the white frost of the morning. Despite the sin of man and the rage of devils there is a sublime sense in which all things from the beginning, since Adam crossed the threshold of Eden even until now, have happened according to the purpose and will of the Lord of Hosts. Prophecy utters her oracles, and history writes her pages, "at thy word," O Lord.

It is wonderful to think of the fisherman of Galilee letting down his net in perfect consonance with all the arrangements of the ages. His net obeys the law that regulates the spheres. His hand consciously does what Arcturus and Orion are doing without thought. This little bell on the Galilean lake rings out in harmony with the everlasting chimes. "At thy word," says Peter, as he promptly obeys, therein repeating the watchword of seas and stars, of winds and worlds. It is glorious thus to be keeping step with the marchings of the armies of the King of kings.

There is another way of working out this thought. "At thy word" has been the password of all good men from the beginning until now. Saints have acted upon these three words and found their marching orders in them. An ark is built on dry land, and the ribald crowd gather about the hoary patriarch, laughing at him; but he is not ashamed, for lifting his face to heaven he says, "I have built this great vessel, O Jehovah, at thy word." Abraham departs the place of his childhood, leaves his family, and goes with Sarah to a land of which he knows nothing, crossing the broad Euphrates and entering upon a country possessed by the Canaanite, in which he roams as a stranger and a sojourner all his days. He dwells in tents with Isaac and Jacob. If any scoff at him for thus renouncing the comforts of settled life, he lifts his calm face to heaven and smilingly answers to the Lord, "It is at thy word." And even when his brow is furrowed and the hot tear is ready to force itself from beneath the patriarch's eyelid as he lifts his hand with the knife to stab Isaac to the heart, if any charge him with murder or think him insane, he lifts the same placid face toward the majesty of the Most High and says, "It is at thy word." At that word he joyfully sheathes the sacrificial knife, for he has proved his willingness to go to the utmost at the word of the Lord his God.

If I were to introduce you to a thousand of the faithful ones who have shown the obedience of faith, in every case they would justify their acts by telling you that they did them "at God's word." Moses lifts his rod in the presence of the haughty Pharaoh, "at thy word," great God! Nor does he lift that rod in vain at Jehovah's word, for thick and heavy fall the plagues upon the children of Ham. They are made to know that God's word returns not to Him void but fulfills His purpose, whether it is of threatening or of promise. See Moses lead the people out of Egypt, the whole host in its myriads! Mark how he has brought them to the Red Sea, where the wilderness shuts them in. The heights frown on either side, and the rattle of Egypt's war chariots is behind. How came Moses so to play the fool and bring them here? Were there no graves in Egypt that thus he brought them forth to die on the Red Sea shore? The answer of Moses is the quiet reflection that he did it at Jehovah's word, and God justifies that word, for the sea opens wide a highway for the elect of God, and they march joyfully through, and with timbrels and dances on the other side they sing unto the Lord who hath triumphed gloriously.

If in later years you find Joshua compassing Jericho and assailing it not with battering rams but only with one great blast of trumpets, his reason is that God has spoken to him by His word. And so right on, for time would fail me to speak of Samson and Jephthah and Barak: these men did what they did at God's word, and doing it, the Lord was with them. Is it bringing things down from the sublime to the ridiculous to talk of Peter and the net that he cast over the side of his little boat? Oh, no. We are ourselves ridiculous when we do not make our own lives sublime by the obedience of faith. Certainly, there may be as much sublimity in casting a net as in building an ark, lifting a rod, or sounding a ram's horn.

It is clear that if it is done in faith, the simplest action of life may be sublimely great. The flash of the wave as it covers Peter's net may be as sublime before the Lord as the glory of the Red Sea billow when it returned in its strength. God who sees a world in a drop sees wonders in the smallest act of faith. Do not, I pray you, think that sublimity lies in masses, to be measured by a scale, so that a mile shall be sublime and an inch shall be absurd. We measure not moral and spiritual things by rods and chains. The common act of fishing at Christ's word links Peter with all the principalities and powers and forces that in all ages have known this as their only law: "He spake, and it was done; he commanded, and it stood fast" (Ps. 33:9). We, too, shall have fellowship with the sublime if we know how to be perfectly obedient to the word of the Lord.

This should be the rule of all Christians for the entirety of their lives—"At thy word." This should direct us in the church and in the world. It should guide us in our spiritual beliefs and in our secular acts—"At thy word." I wish it were so. We hear boastings that the Bible alone is the religion of the Protestants. It is a mere boast. Few

Protestants can honestly repeat the assertion. They have other books to which they pay deference, and other rules and other guides—beyond and above, and even in opposition to, the one Word of God. It should not be so. The power of the Church and the power of the individual to please God shall never be fully known till we get back to the simple yet sublime rule of our text, "At thy word."

This rule has many applications. First, I shall somewhat repeat myself by saying that *it should apply to the affairs of ordinary life. Second, it should apply to matters of spiritual profiting. And third, it should find its chief application in our great life business, which is being fishers of men.*

To All Affairs of Ordinary Life

I mean, first, as to continuance in honest industry. "Let every man abide in the same calling wherein he was called" (1 Cor. 7:20). Many a man in the present difficult crisis is half ready to give up his work and run away from his business because he has toiled all night and taken nothing. Truly, the financial darkness has lasted long and does not yet yield to the dawning, but yet Christians must not murmur or leave their posts. O tried ones, continue to be diligent in your business, still provide things honest in the sight of all men. Labor on in hope. Say just as Peter did, "Nevertheless at thy word I will let down the net." "Except the LORD build the house, they labour in vain that build it" (Ps. 127:1): you know that truth full well. Know this also, that the Lord will not forsake His people. Your best endeavors will not of themselves bring you prosperity; still, do not relax those endeavors. God's word to you is to be strong, gird up the loins of your mind, be sober, and stand fast. Throw not away your shield, cast not away your confidence, but stand steadily in your rank till the tide of battle turns. God has placed you where you are; move not till His providence calls you. Do not run before the cloud. Take down the shutters tomorrow morning and display your goods, and let not despondency drive you to anything rash or unseemly. Say, "Nevertheless at thy word I will let down the net."

If I am speaking to someone who is out of work just now, searching for some place where you can provide bread for yourself and your family, please listen and ponder. If any man does not do his best to provide for his own household, he comes not under a gospel blessing, but he is said to be worse than a heathen man and a publican (1 Tim. 5:8). It is the duty of us all to labor with our hands that which is good, that we may have to give to the needy as well as those dependent on us. If, after you have gone about this city till your feet are blistered, you can find nothing to do, do not sit at home next Monday, sulkily saying, "I will not try again." Apply my text to this painful trial, and yet again set forth in hope, saying with Peter, "We have toiled all the night, and have taken nothing: nevertheless at thy word I will let down the net."

Let men see that a Christian is not readily driven to despair: nay, let them see that when the yoke is made more heavy, the Lord has a secret way of strengthening the backs of His children to bear their burdens. If the Holy Spirit shall make you calmly resolute, you will honor God much more by your happy perseverance than will the politician by his fine speeches or the formalist by his outward show. Common life is the true place in which to prove the truth of godliness and bring glory to God. Not by doing extraordinary works but by the holiness of ordinary life is the Christian known and his religion honored. At God's word hold on even to the end. "Trust in the LORD, and do good; so shalt thou dwell in the land, and verily thou shalt be fed" (Ps. 37:3).

It may be, too, that you have been endeavoring in your daily life to acquire skill in your business and you have not succeeded, or you have tried to acquire more knowledge so that you could better fulfill your vocation, but you have not prospered as you had wished. Do not, therefore, cease from your efforts. Christians must never be lazy. Our Lord Jesus would never have it said that His disciples are a sort of cowards who, if they do not succeed the first time, will never try again. We are to be patterns of all the moral virtues as well as of the spiritual grace. Therefore, at the bidding of the Lord, work on with mind and hand, and look to Jesus for the blessing. "At His word" let down the net once more. He may intend largely to bless you when by trial you have been prepared to bear the benediction.

This applies very closely to those who are laboring hard in the training of children. It may be that with your own children you have not succeeded yet. The boy's spirit may still be wild and proud, and the girl may not yet have yielded to obedience and submission. Or you may be working in the Sunday school or in the public school, trying to impart knowledge and to fashion the youthful mind aright, and you may have been baffled. But if it is your business to teach, do not be overcome. Stand to your work as though you heard Jesus say, "Whatsoever ye do, do it heartily, as to the Lord, and not unto men" (Col. 3:23). Earnestly, then, at His word again let down the net.

I counsel you, dear friend, in everything to which you set your hands, if it is a good thing, do it with all your might; and if it is not a good thing, have nothing to do with it. It may be possible that you are called to teach the age some moral truth. In most generations, individuals have been called to carry out reform and to promote progress. You are bound to love your neighbor as yourself, therefore as you have opportunity, do good to all men (Gal. 6:10). If you have tried and have not won a hearing yet, do not give up your point. If it is a good thing and you are a Christian man, never let it be said that you were afraid or ashamed. I should not like to see our Lord followed by a set of cowards who could not fight the common battles of life. How should such as these become worthy of the lordlier chivalry that wrestles with spiritual wickedness in high places? It is for us to be bravest among the brave in the plains of common life, that when we are summoned to higher fields, where still greater deeds are needed, we may go there trained for the higher service.

Does it seem to you to be a little out of place to be writing in this manner? I do not think so. I notice how in the Old Testament we are told of the sheep and the cattle and the fields and the harvests of good men, and these had to do with their religion. I notice how the prudent woman according to Solomon provided for her household. I observe that we have in the Bible a book of Proverbs, and another called Ecclesiastes, with little spiritual teaching in them but a great deal of good, sound, practical common sense. It is evident to me that the Lord intends that our faith should not be locked up in a pew but should walk the shop and be seen in every walk of life. The great principle of my text fell from the lips of a working man, and to the working man I return it. It was connected with a net and a boat, the implements of his labor, and with these common things I would link it. I would say to all who serve the Lord in this present evil world—in the name of God, if you have anything to do, be not so desponding and despairing as to cease from it, but according to His word, once more go forward in your honest endeavors and, like Peter, say, "I will let down the net." This may prove to be a word in season to some who are weary of the hardness of the times. I shall rejoice if it nerves an arm or cheers a heart. Have faith in God. "Be ye stedfast, unmoveable, always abounding in the work of the Lord" (1 Cor. 15:58).

In Matters of Spiritual Profiting

I write this, first, to those who are *hoping to find salvation*. You have prayed before reading this chapter that the Lord would really bless it to you. Now, mark, I do not understand you at all, because the way of salvation is open to you at this very moment, and it is, "Believe on the Lord Jesus Christ, and thou shalt be saved" (Acts 16:31). You have nothing to wait for, and all your waiting is sinful. If you say you are waiting for the stirring of the pool, I tell you there is no pool to be stirred and no angel to stir it. That pool was dried up long ago, and angels never go that way now. Our Lord Jesus Christ shut up Bethesda when He came and said to the man lying there, "Rise, take up thy bed, and walk" (John 5:8). That is what He says to you. You have no business waiting; but as you are, I earnestly invite you at the word of Christ, "Believe and live." Let down the net once more and let it down this way; say, "My Lord, I believe; help thou mine unbelief"(Mk. 9:24). Breathe a prayer now to Jesus that He would accept you. Submit yourself to Him and ask Him to become now at this moment your Savior. You will be heard. Plenty of fish are waiting to be taken in the net of faith. At the Lord's word let it down.

But I will now address others who have been letting down their nets, in vain, perhaps, in the form of *importunate prayer*. Have you been praying for the conversion of a relative or pleading for some other good thing that you believe to be according to the will of God, and after long pleading—pleading in the night, for your spirit has been sad—are you tempted never to offer that petition anymore? Now then, at Christ's word, who said "that men ought always to pray, and not to faint" (Luke 18:1), let down the net and pray again. Not because the circumstances that surround you are more favorable, but simply because Jesus bids you to continue in prayer, and who knows but that this very time you will meet with success!

Or have you been *searching the Scriptures to find a promise* that suits your case? Do you want to get hold of some good word from God that will cheer you? Shoals of such fish are around your boat; the sea of Scripture is full of them. Fish of promise, I mean, but alas, you cannot catch any of them! Nevertheless, try again. Search the Scriptures again with prayer, and beseech the Holy Spirit to apply a precious portion to your heart, that you may by faith enjoy the sweetness of it. Who knows but you shall this very day obtain your desire and receive a larger blessing than your mind can fully contain, so that in your case also the net shall break through the fullness of the favor.

Or it may be that you have been laboring a long while after *some holy attainment.* You want to conquer a besetting sin, to exercise firmer faith, to exhibit more zeal, and to be more useful, but you have not yet gained your desire. Now, then, since it is the Lord's mind that you should be "perfect in every good work to do his will" (Heb. 13:21), do not cease from your purpose, but at His word let down your net again. Never despair. That temper of yours will be conquered yet; that unbelief of yours will give way to holy faith. Let down the net, and all the graces may yet be taken in it, to be yours for the rest of your life. Only at Christ's word still labor for the best things, and He will give them to you.

Or are you seeking *the nearer presence of Christ* and a nearer fellowship with Him? Are you yearning after a sight of His face—the face that outshines the morning? Do you wish to be brought into His banqueting house to be satiated with His love? And have you cried in vain? Then cry once more, "at his word," for He bids you come to Him. His loving voice invites you to draw near. At His word press forward once again, let down the net once more, and joys await you unspeakable, surpassing all you have experienced before.

Thus you see that there is a just application of the great principle of the text to our spiritual profiting. God help us by His gracious Spirit to carry it out from day to day.

Our Life Business

What is the life business of every Christian here? Is it not soul winning? That we may glorify God by the bringing of others to the faith of Christ is the great object of our remaining here on earth. Otherwise, we should have been caught up to swell the harmony of the heavenly songs. It is expedient for many wandering sheep here below that we should tarry until we have brought them home to the great Shepherd and Bishop of souls.

Our way of winning men for Christ or, to use His own metaphor, our method of catching men, is by letting down the net of the gospel. We have learned no other way of holy fishery. Men with great zeal and little knowledge are inventing ingenious methods for catching men, but for my part I believe in nothing but declaring the story of the love of God to men in Christ Jesus. No new gospel has been committed to us by Jesus, and He has authorized no new way of making it known. Our Lord has called all of us to the work of proclaiming free pardon through His blood to all who believe in Him. Each believer has a warrant to seek the conversion of his fellows. May not every man seek to save his brother from the burning? Must not Jesus smile on any man's endeavor to deliver his neighbor from going down to eternal death? Has He not said, "Let him that heareth say, Come" (Rev. 22:17)? Whoever hears the gospel is to invite others to come to Christ. The word of the Lord is our warrant for keeping to our one work of making known the gospel. It would be a sorry act of mutiny if we were either to be silent or to preach another gospel which is not another. The word of the Lord is a warrant that justifies the man who obeys it. "Where the word of a king is there is power." What higher authority can we need?

"Oh, but," they say, "you should advance to something higher than the mere elementary doctrine of grace and give the people something more in keeping with the progress of the age." We shall not do so while Jesus bids us go into all the world and preach the gospel to every creature. If we do what He tells us, the responsibility of the matter rests no longer with us. Whatever comes of it, we are clear if we have obeyed orders. A servant is not to justify his master's message but to deliver it. This makes it a joy to preach, this doing it "at thy word." Our business is to do what Christ tells us, as Christ tells us, and to do this again and again, so long as we have breath in our bodies. The commanding Word cries ever to us: "Preach the gospel, preach the gospel to every creature!" Our justification for setting forth Christ crucified and incessantly bidding men believe and live lies in that same Word that bade Peter walk the sea and bade Moses fetch water out of a rock.

The result of this preaching will justify Him who commanded it. No man at the last will be able to say to the Savior, "You set your servants an impossible task, and you gave them an instrument to use that was not at all adapted to produce its end." No, but at the closing up of all things it shall be seen that for the salvation of the elect there was nothing better than a crucified Savior, and to make that crucified Savior known there was no better means than the simple proclamation of His Word by honest lips in the power of the Spirit of the Lord. The foolishness of preaching will turn out to be the great proof of the wisdom of God.

You who teach in the school, or you who preach from the pulpit or distribute literature or speak personally to individuals, you need not be afraid but what Wisdom will exonerate herself from all charges and vindicate her own methods. You may be called a fool today for preaching the gospel, but that accusation, like rust on a sword, will wear off as you use the weapon in the wars of the Lord. The preaching of the Word soon puts down all clamors against itself. Those clamors mainly arise because it is not preached. No one calls the gospel weak where it is smiting right and left like a great two-handed sword. Our reply to the outcry about the failure of the pulpit is to get into it and preach with the Holy Ghost sent down from heaven.

Indeed, this word of Christ, whereby He gives us His warrant for letting down the net, is such that it amounts to a command, and it will leave us guilty if we do not obey. Suppose Simon Peter had said, "We have toiled all the night, and have taken nothing; and therefore, notwithstanding thy word, I will not let down the net"? Then Simon Peter had been guilty of disobedience to his Lord. What shall I say to any of my fellow Christians who profess to be called of God and to be Christ's disciples and yet never do let down the net? Is it so that you are doing nothing for the truth? Do you never disseminate the gospel? Is it so that you call yourselves lights of the world and yet never shine? Are you sowers of the seed and yet forget that you have a seed basket? Am I addressing someone who is in this respect wasting his life? Is it professedly your life's object to be fishers of men and yet you have never cast a net or even helped to draw one on shore? Are you mocking God by a fruitless profession that you never try to make fruitful?

What shall be said of the man to whom the Lord gives the command that he shall make known the glad tidings of salvation from eternal misery and yet he is sinfully silent? The great Physician has entrusted you with the medicine that heals the sick; you see them die about you, but you never speak of the remedy! The great King has given you the meal with which to feed the hungry, and you lock the storehouse door, while the crowds are starving in your streets. Is not this a crime that may well make a man of God weep over you? This great London of ours is growing heathenish to the very core, and yet our Lord has given the gospel into the hands of His churches.

What can be the reason of the indifference of the godly? If we keep this gospel to ourselves, certainly coming ages will condemn us as cruel to our posterity. Succeeding generations will point to our era and say, "What sort of men were these that had the light and shut it up in a dark lantern?" In a century to come, when others shall stand in this city and walk these streets, they will say, "A curse upon the memory of the ministers and people who failed in their duty, who came to the kingdom in a solemn time but never realized their calling, and so missed the end and object of their being!" May we be spared from such a calamity as this. Yes, we have a warrant for laboring to spread the truth of God. And more than a warrant; we have a statute from the throne, a peremptory command, and it is woe to us if we preach not the gospel.

This warrant from Christ is one that—if we are in the state of heart of Simon Peter—will be omnipotent with us. It was very powerful with Simon Peter. For, observe, he was *under the influence of a great disappointment*, yet he laid down the net. "We have toiled all the night." Some say, "We have had all this gospel preaching, we have had all these revivals, and nothing has come of it." When was that? I hear a good deal of this talk, but what are the facts? "Oh," you say, "you know we have had a great deal of revival a little while ago." I do not know anything of the sort. We have had flashes of light here and there, but comparatively so little that it is a pity to make so much of it.

Considering the little that has ever been done for it, however, the spread of the gospel has been marvelous. Look at the gospel work at the present moment in India! People say that the Christian faith is not spreading. I say that it is spreading wonderfully compared with the labor expended and the sacrifice made. If in that land you spend a penny and get a thousand pounds, you have no right to say, "What is that? We want a million." If your desires are thus exacting, prove their sincerity by corresponding action. Increase your outlay. The harvest is wonderful considering the little seed, but if you wish for more sheaves, sow more. The Church has had an enormous return for what little she has done. In England there have been partial revivals, but to what have they amounted? A flash of light has been seen in a certain district, but darkness has still remained supreme over the length and breadth of the country. The papers have reported a great work in a certain spot, but if the papers had reported the places where there has been no revival, we should have had a different view of things!

The fact is that the Church has scarcely ever been in a state of universal revival since the day of Pentecost. There has been a partial moving among Christians every now and then, but the whole mass throughout has never burned and flamed with the earnestness that the great cause demands. Oh, that the Lord would set the whole Church on fire! We have no cause whatever for disappointment. In proportion to the little effort put out, great things have come to us. Therefore let us get to our nets again and say no more about the night in which we have toiled.

But next, this command in Peter *overcame his love of ease*. Evidently he was tired when he said, "We have toiled all the night."

Fishing is hard work, especially when no fish are caught. It is natural to wish to be excused from further toil when you are already weary with unrewarded labor. I have heard some Christians say, "You know I had my time in the Sunday school years ago, and then I used to work too much for my strength." No doubt their youthful efforts were stupendous in the remote ages of their youthful zeal; we can hardly imagine what they must have been like, for no relic remains to assist our conceptions. At this time they feel authorized to take things easy, for they owe no more to their Lord, or at least they do not intend to pay any more. Is it so that any one of us can cease from service when it is plain that we do not cease from receiving mercy at the Lord's hands? Are we not ashamed of the case when it is plainly put? "Take it easy." Yes, soon, very soon, we shall take it easy, for there will be rest enough in the grave. Just now, while souls of men are perishing, to relax our efforts is wickedness. No, no, Peter, although you may be now in a dripping sweat through having toiled all night, you must get at it again. He does so. The night's work is nothing; he must work in the day, too, if he is to catch fish.

Moreover, the command of Christ was so supreme over Peter that he was *not held back by carnal reason*, for reason would say, "If you could not catch fish in the night, you will certainly not do so in the day." Night was the special time for taking fish on the Gennesaret lake and, by day, when the garish sun was lighting up the waves and letting the fish see every single mesh of the net, they were not likely to come into it. But when Christ commands, the most unlikely time is likely, and the most unpromising sphere becomes hopeful. No act is out of season when Christ commands it. If He says, "Go," go at once, without deliberation. "Say not ye, There are yet four months, and then cometh harvest?...the fields...are white already to harvest" (John 4:35). Peter lets down the net at once, and wisely does he act at Christ's word.

The lesson to you and to me is this: Let us do as Peter did and let down the net *personally*, for the apostle said, "I will let down the net." Brother, cannot you do something yourself with your own heart, lips, and hands? Sister, cannot you do something yourself with your own gentle spirit? Do not wait for others. You had better get to work yourself as Peter did.

And you had better do it *at once*, for Peter immediately let down the net, as soon as ever he had launched out into the deep. You may never have another opportunity. Your zeal may have evaporated, or your life may be over. Peter, however, let down only one net, and there was the pity of it. If John and James and all the rest had let down their nets, the result would have been much better. "Why?" say you. Because, through there being only one net, that net was overstrained and broke. If all the nets had been used, they might have taken more fish, and no net would have been broken. Had there been more nets and boats, they might have buoyed up the whole of the fish. As it was, many fish were lost through the breaking of the net. If a church can be so awakened that each individual gets to work in the power of the Holy Spirit and all the individuals combine, how many souls will be captured for Jesus! Multitudes of souls are lost to the blessed gospel because of our broken nets, and the nets get broken because we are not well united in the holy service, and by our unwisdom cause loss to our Master's cause. Ministers need not become worn out with labor if all would take their share. One boat would not begin to sink if the other boats took a part of the blessed load.

I hope I have made you ready to accept the following directory of service drawn from the text. The way in which to serve God is to do it at His word. I pray that none of us may sink into serving the Lord as a matter of routine. May we never fall to serving Him in our own strength. We must preach, teach, and labor in His name because we hear Him bidding us do it. We must act at His word. If this were the case, we should work with much more faith, with much more earnestness, and with much more likelihood of success. It is a blessed thing to see Christ sitting in the boat while you cast out the net. If you catch a glimpse of His approving smile as He watches you, you will work heartily. We must labor in entire dependence upon Him, not preaching or teaching because in our judgment it is the right thing to do—Peter did not think so—but because Jesus gives the word, and His word is law. You may not work because you have any expectation of success from the excellence of your work or from the nature of the people among whom you labor but because Jesus has given you the word. You stand there doing a thing that critics sneer at as absurd, but you do it in all confidence, believing that it must be wise because Jesus bids you do it.

I remember well how some of our brethren used to talk to us. They said, "You preach the gospel to dead sinners, bidding them repent and believe. You might just as well shake a handkerchief over a grave and bid the corpse come out of it." Exactly so. They spoke the truth, but then I would delight to go and shake a handkerchief over graves and bid the dead live if Jesus bade me do so. I should expect to see the cemetery crack and heave from end to end if I were sent on such an errand by the Lord. I would accept the duty joyfully. The more absurd the wise men of our age make the gospel out to be, and the more they show that it is powerless to produce the end designed, the more will we persevere in our old method of preaching Jesus crucified. Our resolves are not to be shaken by that mode of reasoning. We never did draw our argument for preaching the gospel from the work itself but from the orders given us to do it, and we would rather be acting upon the responsibility of Christ than upon our own. I would rather be a fool and do what Christ tells me than be the wisest man of the modern world and despise the word of the Lord. I would rather lay the responsibility of my life at the feet of Him who bids me live according to His Word than seek out an object in life for myself and feel that the responsibility rested on my own shoulders. Let us be willing to be under orders to Christ, willing to persevere under difficulties, willing to begin anew in His service from this very hour.

If all you have is very little—just a few loaves and fishes—use that properly, and you will do your Master service. And in due time, when God wants you, He knows where to find you. You need not put an advertisement in the paper. He knows the street you live in and the number on the door. You need not go and push yourself to the front, for the Lord will bring you to the front when He wants you. I hope that you do not want to get there if He does not want you. Depend upon it, should you push forward when you are not required, He will put you back again. Oh, for grace to work on unobserved, to have your one talent, your five loaves and two fishes, and only to be noticed when the hour suggests that need and the need makes a loud call for you. We have thus seen, first of all, the loaves and fishes in the desert, quite unnoticed, but put there by providence; and we now behold them by that same providence, thrust into prominence.

Chapter Five

The Lad's Loaves
in the Lord's Hands

Jesus took the loaves—John 6:11.

LOOK, THERE ARE THE PEOPLE! Five thousand of them, as hungry as hunters, and they all need to have food given to them, for they cannot travel to buy it! And here is the provision! Five thin wafers—and those of barley, more fit for horses than for men—and two little anchovies, by way of a relish! Five thousand people and five little biscuits to feed them! The proportion is ridiculous: if each one should have only the tiniest crumb, there would not be nearly enough. In like manner, there are millions of people in London, and only a handful of wholehearted Christians earnestly desiring to see the city converted to Christ. There are more than a thousand millions of men in this round world, and oh, so few missionaries breaking to them the bread of life. It is almost as few workers for the millions as were these five barley cakes for those five thousand! The problem is a very difficult one.

The contrast between the supply and the demand would have struck us much more vividly if we had been in that crowd at Bethseda than it does nearly two thousand years later and merely hearing about it. But the Lord Jesus was capable of meeting the emergency. None of the people went away without sharing in His bounty. They were all filled. Our blessed Master, now that He has ascended into the heavens, has more rather than less power. He is not baffled because of our lack but can even now use our inadequacies to accomplish His own glorious purposes. Therefore let no man's heart fail him. Do not despair of the evangelization of London or think it hopeless that the gospel should be preached in all nations for a testimony unto them. Have faith in God, who is in Christ Jesus. Have faith in the compassion of the Great Mediator. He will not desert the people in their spiritual need, any more than He failed that hungry throng in their temporal need long ago.

We will now look at these biscuits and sardines, which were a truly insufficient source to begin with, a very small capital indeed on which to conduct the business of feeding five thousand persons. I shall say of these loaves and fishes, first, that *they had a previous history* before being mentioned in our text. Second, when we get to our text, we shall find these little things *in a very grand position*—"Jesus took the loaves." And therefore, third, *they will have an after-history* that is well worthy of being noted. When things get into Christ's hands, they are in the very focus of miracles.

The Loaves and Fishes Had a Previous History

Andrew said to Jesus, "There is a lad here, which hath five barley loaves, and two small fishes" (John 6:9).

Notice, first, then, *the providence of God in bringing the lad there.* We do not know his name and are not told anything concerning his parentage. Was he a little peddler, who thought that he could make some money by selling a few loaves and fishes, and had he nearly sold out? Or was he a boy that the apostles had employed to carry this slender provision for the use of Jesus and His friends? We do not know much about him, but he was the right boy in the right place that day. Whatever his name was, it did not matter. He had the barley loaves and fishes upon which the people were to be fed. Christ never is in need but He has somebody at hand to supply that need. Have faith in the providence of God. What made the boy bring the loaves and fishes, I do not know. Boys often do unaccountable things, but bring the loaves and fishes he did. And God, who understands the ideas and motives of lads and takes account even of barley loaves and fishes, had appointed that boy to be there. Again I say, believe in the providence of God.

Mr. Stanley tells us that when he came out of that long journey of his through the African forest, I think after a hundred and sixty days of walking in darkness, and found himself at last where he could see the sun, he felt that there was a special providence of God that had taken care of him. I am very glad that Mr. Stanley felt that it was the hand of God that had brought him out of the dreadful shade. But I do not need to go to Africa to learn that we are beset behind and before by His goodness. Many of us have felt a special providence of God in our own homes. We have seen His hand in connection with our own children. Yea, every day we are surrounded by tokens of His care. "Whoso is wise, and will observe these things, even they shall understand the lovingkindness of the LORD" (Ps. 107:43). "I am sure God took care of me," said one, "for as I was going along a certain street, I slipped on a piece of orange peel and had what might have been a serious fall. Yet I was not hurt in the least." To which his friend replied, "I am sure God has taken care of *me*, for I have walked along that street hundreds of times, and have never slipped on a piece of orange peel, or on anything else." So often God draws near to us in common life.

Let us also believe in His providence with regard to the Church of Christ. God will never desert His people. He will find men when He wants them. Thus it has ever been in the history of the saints, and thus it shall ever be. Before the Reformation there were many educated men who knew something of Christ's gospel. But they said that it was a pity to make a noise, and so these men communed with one another and with Christ very quietly. What was needed was some rough, bullheaded fellow who would blurt the gospel out and upset the old state of things. Where could he be found? There was a monk named Luther, who, while reading his Bible, suddenly stumbled on the doctrine of justification by faith. Luther was God's man for the hour. Yet when he went to a dear brother in the Lord and told him how he felt, Luther's friend said to him, "Go back to thy cell, and pray and commune with God, and hold thy tongue." But Luther had a tongue that he could not hold and that nobody else could hold, and he began to speak with it the truth that had made a new man of him.

The God that made Luther knew what He was at when He made him. He put within Luther a great burning fire that could not be restrained, and it burst forth and set the nations on a blaze. Never despair about providence. There sits at this moment somewhere in a chimney corner in the country a man who will turn the current of unbelief and win back the churches to the old gospel. God has never come to a point of distress as to His truth but that suddenly one came forward, a David with a sling and a stone, or a Samson with a jawbone, or a Shamgar with an ox-goad, who put to rout the adversaries of the Lord. "There is a lad here." The providence of God had sent him.

Next, *this lad with his loaves was brought into notice.* When they were searching for all the provisions in the company, this obscure boy, who never would have been heard of otherwise, was brought to the front because he had his little basket of biscuits. Andrew found him out, and he came and said to Jesus, "There is a lad here, which hath five barley loaves, and two small fishes." So rest assured that, if you have the Bread of Life about you and you are willing to serve God, you need not be afraid that obscurity will ever prevent your doing it. "Nobody knows me," says one. It is not a very desirable thing that anybody should know you. Those of us who are known to everybody would be very glad if we were not, for there is little comfort in it. The person who can work away for his Master, with nobody to see him but his Master, is the happiest of men. "I have only one hundred people to preach to," said a country pastor to me. I replied, "If you give a good account of those hundred, you have quite enough to do."

If all you have is very little—just a few loaves and fishes—use that properly, and you will do your Master service. And in due time, when God wants you, He knows where to find you. You need not put an advertisement in the paper. He knows the street you live in and the number on the door. You need not go and push yourself to the front, for the Lord will bring you to the front when He wants you. I hope that you do not want to get there if He does not want you. Depend upon it, should you push forward when you are not required, He will put you back again. Oh, for grace to work on unobserved, to have your one talent, your five loaves and two fishes, and only to be noticed when the hour suggests that need and the need makes a loud call for you. We have thus seen, first of all, the loaves and fishes in the desert, quite unnoticed, but put there by providence; and we now behold them by that same providence, thrust into prominence.

When brought into notice, the loaves and fishes did not fare very well. *They were judged insufficient for the purpose*, for Andrew said, "What are they among so many?" (John 6:9). The boy's candle seemed to be quite snuffed out. So small a stock—what could be the use of that? I dare say that you have had Satan saying to you, "What is the use of your trying to do anything?" To you, dear mother, with a family of children, he has whispered, "You cannot serve God." He knows very well that by sustaining grace you can, and he is afraid of how well you can serve God if you bring up those dear children in His fear. Satan says to the Sunday school teacher over yonder, "You have not much ability. What can you do?" Ah, dear friend! He is afraid of what you can do, and if you will only do what you can do, God will help you to do what now you cannot do. While the devil is afraid of even the little that you can do now, many a child of God seems to side with Satan in despising the day of small things. "What are they among so many?" So few, so poor, so devoid of talent, what can any of us hope to do? Disdained, even by the disciples, it is small wonder if we are held in contempt by the world. The things that God will honor, man must first despise. You run the gauntlet of the derision of men, and afterward you come out to be used of God.

Though seemingly inadequate to feed the multitude, these loaves and fishes would have been quite enough for the boy's supper, yet *he appears to have been quite willing to part with them*. The disciples would not have taken them from him by force, and the Master would not have allowed it. The lad willingly gave them up to be the commencement of the great feast. Somebody might have said, "John, you know that you will soon be able to eat those five cakes and two little fishes. Better keep them away from the others. Every man for himself." Is it not a good rule, "Take care of number one"? Yes, but the boy whom God uses will not be selfish. Am I speaking to some young Christian to whom Satan says, "Make money first, and serve God later. Stick to business, and get on. Then, after that, you can act like a Christian and give some money away."

Let such a one remember the barley loaves and the fishes. If that lad had really wisely studied his own interests instead of merely yielding with a generous impulse to the demand of Christ, he would have done exactly what he did, for if he had kept the loaves, he would have eaten them, and there would have been an end of them. But now that he brings them to Christ, all those thousands of people are fed, and he gets as much himself as he would have had if he had eaten his own stock. And then, in addition, he gets a share out of the twelve baskets full of fragments that remain. Anything that you take away from self and give to Christ is well invested. It will often bring in ten thousand percent. The Lord knows how to give such a reward to an unselfish man, that he will feel that he who saves his life loses it, but he who is willing even to lose his life, and the bread that sustains it, is the man who, after all, gets truly saved.

This, then, is the history of these loaves. They were sent there through God's providence by a lad who was sought out and brought into notice. The boy's supply was despised, but he was willing to give it, whether it was despised or not. He would yield it to his Lord. Do you see what I am driving at? I want to get ahold of some of you who think that you have very little ability and say to you, "Come, and bring it to Jesus." We want you. Times are hard. The people are famishing. Though nobody seems to need you, yet be bold to come out. Who knows but that, like Queen Esther, you may have come to the kingdom for such a time as this? God may have brought you where you are to make use of you for the converting of thousands, but you must be converted yourself first. Christ will not use you unless you are first His own. You must yield yourself up to Him and be saved by His precious blood and then, after that, come and yield up to Him all the little talent that you may have. Pray that Jesus Christ will make as much use of you as He did of the lad with the five barley cakes.

The Barley Cakes Got into a Grand Position

The text says, "Jesus took the loaves." He took them into His own hands. From the trembling hands of the boy or from his little basket, they were transferred to the blessed hands that one day would bear the nail prints. This may teach us several lessons.

First, *they were now associated with Jesus Christ.* Henceforth, those loaves do not so much suggest the thought of the lad's sacrifice as of the Savior's power. Is it not a wonderful thing that Christ, the living God, should associate Himself with our feebleness, with our lack of talent, with our ignorance, with our little faith? And yet He does so. If we are not associated with Him, we can do nothing, but when we come into living touch with Him, we can do all things. Those barley loaves in Christ's hands become pregnant with food for all the multitude. Out of His hands they are nothing but barley cakes, but in His hands, associated with Him, they are in contact with omnipotence. Have you that love the Lord Jesus Christ thought of bringing all that you possess to Him, that it may be associated with Him? There is that brain of yours; it can be associated with the teachings of His Spirit. There is that heart of yours; it can be warmed with the love of God. There is that tongue of yours; it can be touched with the live coal from off the altar. There is that manhood of yours; it can be perfectly consecrated by association with Christ.

Hear the tender command of the Lord, "Bring them hither to me," and your whole life will be transformed. I do not say that every man of ordinary ability can rise to high ability by being associated with Christ through faith. But I do say this, that his ordinary ability, in association with Christ, will become sufficient for the occasion to which God in providence has called him. I know that you have been praying and saying, "I have not this, and I cannot do that." Stop numbering your deficiencies. Bring what you have and let all that you are—body, soul, and spirit—be associated with Christ. Although He will not bestow upon you new faculties, the faculties you have will have new power, for they will come into a new condition toward Him. And what may not be hoped for by association with such wisdom and might?

Further, *they were transferred to Christ.* A moment ago they belonged to this lad, but now they belong to Christ. "Jesus took the loaves." He has taken possession of them, and they are His property. Do you mean what you say when you declare that you have given yourself to Christ? If you have made a full transfer, therein will lie great power for usefulness. But do not people often say, "If I might make some reserve"? "What meaneth then this bleating of the sheep in mine ears, and the lowing of the oxen which I hear?" (1 Sam. 15:14). What about the extra thousand that you put in the funds the other day? What about the money saved up for a new outfit? Oh, that we had more real putting of the loaves into Christ's hands! The time that you have not used for self but have given to Christ. The knowledge that you have not stored as in a reservoir but have given to Christ. The ability that you have not wielded for the world but have yielded to Christ. Your influence and position, your money and home, all put into Christ's hands and reckoned to be not your own but to be His henceforth. This is the way in which London's need will be met and the world's hunger will be satisfied. But we are staggered at the very outset by the lack of this complete dedication of everything to Christ.

What is better still, as these loaves were given to Jesus, so *they were accepted by Jesus.* They were not only dedicated but also consecrated. Jesus took the five barley loaves and the two little fishes, and in doing so, He seemed to say, "These will do for me." As the Revised Version has it, "Jesus *therefore* took the loaves." Was there any reason why He should? Yes, because they were brought to Him, they were willingly presented to Him, there was a need of them, and He could work with them; "therefore" He took the loaves. Children of God, if Christ has ever made use of you, you have often stood and wondered how the Lord could accept you; but there was a "therefore" in it. He saw that you were willing to win souls. He saw the souls needed winning, and He used you, even you. Am I not now writing to some who might be of great service if they yielded themselves to Christ and Christ accepted them and they became accepted in the Beloved? Only five barley cakes, but Jesus accepted them. Only two small fishes, brought by a little lad, but the great Christ accepted them, and they became His own.

What is better still, *these loaves and fishes were blessed by Christ* as He lifted up His eyes and gave thanks to the Father for them. Think of it! For five little cakes and two small fish, Christ gave thanks to the Father. What looked like apparently a meager cause for praise, Jesus knew what He could make of them and therefore gave thanks for what they would presently accomplish. "God loves us," says Augustine, "for what we are becoming." Christ gave thanks for these trifles because He saw whereunto they would grow. Do you not think that having thanked the Father, He also thanked the boy? And in later years, these words of gratitude would be ample recompense for such a tiny deed. Like the woman who cast in the two pennies to the treasury, the lad gave his all and doubtless was commended for the gift.

Though high in glory today, Christ is still grateful when such offerings are made to Him. He still thanks His Father when, with timid, trembling hands, we offer to Him our best, our all, however small. His heart still is gladdened when we bring Him our scanty store that it may be touched by His dear hand and blessed by His gracious lips. He loves us, not for what we are but for what He will yet make us. He blesses our offerings, not for their worth but because His power will yet make them worthy of His praise. May the Lord thus bless every talent that you have! May He bless your memory; may He bless your understanding; may He bless your voice; may He bless your heart; may He bless your head; may He bless you all and evermore! When He puts a blessing into the little gift and into the little grace that we have, good work begins and goes on to perfection.

When the loaves had been blessed, *they were increased by Christ.* Peter takes one, begins to break it, and as he breaks it, he has always as much in his hand as he started with. "Here, take a bit of fish, friend," says he. He gives a whole fish to that man, and he has a whole fish left. So he gives it to another, and another, and another, and goes on scattering the bread and scattering the fish everywhere, as quickly as he can. When he is done, he has his hands just as full of fish and as full of bread as ever. If you serve God, you will never run dry. He who gives you something to say one Sunday will give you something to say another Sunday. For thirty-seven years I have ministered to this same church and congregation, and every time that I have preached, I have said all that I knew.

Some very learned brethren are like the great tun of

Heidelberg; they can hold so much wine that there is enough to swim in, but they put in a tap somewhere up at the top, and you never get much out. Mine is a very small barrel indeed, but the tap is down as low as it can be. You can get more liquor out of a small tub if you empty it than you can out of a big vat if you are only permitted to draw a little from the top.

This boy gave all his loaves and all his fish—not much, truly— but Christ multiplied it. Be like him, give your all. Do not think of reserving some for another occasion. If you are a preacher, do not think of what you will preach about the next time. Think of what you are going to preach about now. It is always enough to get one sermon at a time. If you get a lot piled away somewhere, there will be a stale odor about them. Even the manna that came down from heaven bred worms and stank. So will your best sermons, even if the message is God-given. And if it does not come down from heaven but comes from your own brain, it will go bad still more quickly. Tell the people about Christ. Lead them to Jesus, and do not trouble about what you will say next time. But wait till next time comes, and it shall be given you in the same hour what you shall speak.

Mark once more: when Jesus took the loaves, it was not only to multiply but also to dispose of them. *They were distributed by Christ.* He did not believe in multiplication unless it was attended by division. Christ's additions mean subtraction, and Christ's subtractions mean additions. He gives that we may give away. He multiplied as soon as the disciples began to distribute, and when the distribution ended, the multiplication ended. Oh, for grace to go on distributing! If you have received the truth from Christ, tell it out! God will whisper it in your ear, and tell it in; but if you stop the telling out, if you cease the endeavor to bless others, it may be that God will no more bless you or grant you again the communion of His face.

Putting all this together, if we all would bring our loaves and fishes to the Lord Jesus Christ, He would take them and make them wholly His own. Then, when He should have blessed them, He would multiply them, and He would bid us distribute them, and we could yet meet the needs of London, and the needs of the whole world even to the last man. A Christ who could feed five thousand can feed five million. There is no limit. When once you get a miracle, you may as well have a great one. Whenever I find the critics paring down miracles, it always seems to me to be a very poor work. If it is a miracle, it is a miracle, and if you are in for a penny, you may as well be in for a pound. If you can believe that Christ can feed fifty, then you can believe that He can feed five hundred, five thousand, five million, five hundred million, if it so pleases Him.

Thus have I tried to stir up God's people to believe in the Lord and consecrate themselves to Him. But some of you are saying, "He is not writing to me." No, I am not writing *to* you, but I am writing *for* you. For if God's people begin to be roused, they will soon look after you. You will have somebody asking you about your soul before you get out of church. During the week, if you meet some of them, they will be troubling you, rousing up your conscience, and making you feel what an awful thing it is to live without Christ. I hope that it will be so. You who do not love my Lord, what are you? Paul said that you would be Anathema Maranatha (1 Cor. 16:22)— cursed at His coming! I pray you, do not rest easy while that may be your portion. You are the people whom we want to feed, you are the people whom we want to bless. Oh, that God in His mercy would but bless you! We do not ask to have the honor of it. We would be willing to have it quite unknown who it was that brought you to the Savior, so long as you did but come to Him. May the Lord in mercy bring you!

The Loaves and Fishes Had an After-History

The loaves got into Christ's hands. What was the result?

First, *a great deal of misery was removed* by the lad's basketful of barley cakes. Those poor people were famished. They had been with Christ all day and had had nothing to eat. Had they been dispersed as they were, tired and hungry, many of them would have fainted by the way. Perhaps some would even have died. Oh, what would we give if we might but alleviate the misery of this world! I remember the Earl of Shaftesbury saying, "I should like to live longer. I cannot bear to go out of the world while there is so much misery in it." And you know how that dear saint of God laid himself out to look after the poor and the helpless and the needy all his days. Perhaps you have never awakened yet to the idea that if you were to bring your little all to Christ, He could make use of it in alleviating the misery of many a wounded conscience and that awful misery that will come upon men if they die unforgiven and stand before the judgment bar of God without a Savior. Yes, God can make you the spiritual father of many.

As I look back upon my own history, little did I dream when first I opened my mouth for Christ, in a very humble way, that I should have the honor of bringing thousands to Jesus. Blessed, blessed be His name! He has the glory of it. But I cannot help thinking that there must be many others, such as I was, whom He may call by His grace to do service for Him. When I had a letter sent to me by the deacons of the church at New Park Street to come up to London to preach, I told them that they had made a mistake, that I was a lad of nineteen years of age, happy among a very poor and lowly people in Cambridgeshire, who loved me, and that I did not imagine that they could mean that I was to preach in London. But they said that they knew all about it, and I must come. Ah, what a story it has been since then of the goodness and lovingkindness of the Lord!

Perhaps these words come to some brother who has never yet laid hold of the idea that God can use him. You must not think that God picks out all the very choice and particularly fine persons. It is not so in the Bible. Some of those that He took were very rough people. Even the first apostles were mostly fishermen. Paul was an educated man, but he was like one born out of due time. The rest of the apostles were not so, but God used them. And it still pleases God, by the base things and things that are not, to bring to nought the things that are.

I do not want you to think highly of yourself. Your cakes are only five, and they are barley, and poor barley at that; and your fish are very small, and there are only two of them. I do not want you to think much of them, but think much of Christ and believe that whoever you may be, if He thought it worth His while to buy you with His blood and is willing to make some use of you, it is surely worth your while to come and bring yourself and all that you have to Him who is thus graciously ready to accept you. Put everything into His hands and let it be said of you, "And Jesus took the loaves." It is a part of the history of the loaves that they alleviated a great mass of misery.

Next, *Jesus was glorified*, for the people said, "He is a prophet." The miracle of the loaves carried them back to the wilderness and to the miracle of the manna. They remembered that Moses had said, "The LORD thy God will raise up unto thee a Prophet from the midst of thee, of thy brethren, like unto me" (Deut. 18:15). For this Deliverer they longed, and as the bread increased, so grew their wonder, until in the swelling cakes they saw the finger of God, and said, "This is of a truth that prophet that should come into the world" (John 6:14). That little lad became, by his loaves and fishes, the revealer of Christ to all the multitude. And who can tell, if you give your loaves to Christ, whether thousands may not recognize Him as the Savior because of it? Christ is still known in the breaking of bread. But the people went further with reference to Christ after they had been fed by the loaves and fishes. They concluded that He was a prophet, and they began whispering among themselves, "Let us make Him a king."

In a better sense than the text implies, I would to God that you and I, though humbly and feebly, might serve Christ till people said, "Christ is a prophet. Let us make Him a king." This message I offer my Master if He will be pleased to accept it, though it is but a barley cake, and I pray that by it some may take Jesus Christ to be their King. Oh, that He had a throne in the hearts of many whom He shall feed at this time with the bread of heaven! Do you wish to glorify Christ? Here is the way. Bring your loaves and fishes to Christ, that He may use them in His divine commissariat, and then He shall be magnified in the eyes of all the people.

When the feast was finished, *there were fragments to be gathered*. This also is a part of the history of the loaves—they were not lost. They were eaten, but they were still there. People were filled with them, but yet there was more of them left than when the feast began. Each disciple had a basketful to carry back to his Master's feet. Give yourself to Christ, and when you have used yourself for

His glory, you will be more able to serve Him than you are now. You shall find your little stock grow as you spend it. Remember John Bunyan's picture of the man who had a roll of cloth. The man unrolled it and cut off some more, and the more he cut it, the longer it grew. Upon which Bunyan remarks, "There was a man, and some did count him mad; The more he gave away, the more he had." It is certainly so with talent and ability and with grace in the heart. The more you use it, the more there is of it. It is often so with gold and silver: the wealth of the liberal man increases, while the miser grows poor. We have an old proverb, which is as true as it is suggestive: "Drawn wells have the sweetest waters." So, if you keep continually drawing on your mind, your thoughts will get sweeter; and if you continue to draw on your strength, your strength will get to be more mighty through God. The more you do, the more you may do, by the grace of the Ever-blessed One!

Last of all, it came to pass, that *these loaves had a record made about them.* There is many a loaf that has gone to a king's table and yet never been chronicled. But this boy's five cakes and two little fishes have got into all four of the gospels. To make quite sure that we should never forget how much God can do with little things, this story is told four times over, and it is the only one of Christ's miracles that has such an abundant record.

As a practical issue, let us now put it to the test. You who have lately joined the Church, do not be long before you try to do something for Christ. You who have for a long time been trusting Christ and yet never begun to work, arouse yourselves to attempt some service for His sake. The aged and sick can still find something to do. Perhaps, at the last, it will be found that the persons whom we might have excused on account of illness or weakness or poverty are the people who have done the most. That, at least, is my observation. I find that if there is a really good work done, it is usually done by an invalid or by somebody who might very properly have said, "I pray You, have me excused." How is it that so many able-bodied and gifted Christians seem to be so slow in the Master's service? The Lord set you all to work with the conversion of others as your object!

If you are Christ's servant, take a sheet of paper and write down, "Lord, I bring my loaves and fishes to You." If you are not

Christ's, confess the awful truth to yourself and face it. I wish that you would make a record of it in black and white, putting down both name and date, "I am not Christ's." Take a good look at it, try to grasp what it means to withhold yourself from Him who loves you and waits to save, and then ask yourself why you are not His. The Lord bless every one of you, wherever you may be! We shall all meet in the day of judgment. May you and I meet without fear there, to sing to the sovereign grace of God that saved us from the wrath to come and helped us while we were here to bring our little and put it into Christ's hands! The Lord be with you!

*I*nsensibility has seized upon many, and a proud conceit. They are full of sin, and yet they talk of self-righteousness. They are weak and can do nothing, yet they boast of their ability. They are not conscious of their true condition, and hence they have no desire to seek a cure. How should they desire healing when they do not believe that they are diseased? How sad that beneath the ruddy cheek of morality there should lurk the fatal illness of enmity to God! How horrible to be healthy on the outside and leprous within! Are there not many who can talk freely about religion and seem right with God, and yet in the secret of their hearts they are the victims of an insincerity and a lack of truth that fatally undermine the life of their profession. They are not what they seem to be. A secret sin drains away the lifeblood of their religion. May the Holy Spirit show us the fatal nature of our soul's disease, for this, I trust, would lead to the making of a firm resolve to find salvation, if salvation is to be had.

Chapter Six

Cured At Last

And a woman having an issue of blood twelve years, which had spent all her living upon physicians, neither could be healed of any, Came behind him, and touched the border of his garment: and immediately her issue of blood stanched—Luke 8:43–44.

THOUGH I TAKE LUKE's statement as text, I shall constantly refer to the version of the same story that we find in Mark 5:25–29. Here we discover one of the Lord's hidden ones: a case not to be publicly described because of its secret sorrow. We have a woman of few words and much shame. Her physical problems subjected her to grievous penalties according to the ceremonial law. There is a terrible chapter in the book of Leviticus concerning such a case as hers. She was unclean—everything that she sat upon and all who touched it shared in the defilement, so that in addition to her continual weakness, she was made to feel herself an outcast under the ban of the law. This created, no doubt, a great loneliness of spirit and made her wish to hide herself from others.

In the narrative before us, she did not speak a word until the Savior drew it out of her, for her own lasting good. She acted very practically and promptly, but she was a silent seeker. She would have preferred to have remained in obscurity, if it could have been. Some people belong to the great company of the timid and trembling ones. If courage before others is needed to secure salvation, it would be very difficult for them, for they shrink from notice and are ready to die of shame because of their secret grief. Cowper's hymn describes their inward feelings when it says of the woman:

> Conceal'd amid the gathering throng
> She would have shunn'd Thy view,
> And if her faith was firm and strong,
> Had strong misgivings too.

Such plants grow in the shade and shrink from the light of the sun. The nature of their sorrows forces them into solitary self-communion. Oh, that the Lord may heal such at this hour!

The immediate cure of this woman is the more remarkable because it was a wayside miracle. The Savior was on the road to restore the daughter of Jairus (Luke 8:42). This woman's healing was an extra of grace, a sort of over-splash of the great fountain of mercy. The cup of our Lord's power was full—full to the brim—and He was carrying it to the house of the ruler of the synagogue. This poor creature did but receive a drop that He spilt on the way. We do well if, when going upon some errand of love, we concentrate all our energy upon it and do it well in the end. But not only could the Savior perform one great marvel, He could work another as a sort of byplay incidentally on the road. The episodes of the Lord Jesus are as beautiful as the main run of His life's poem. Oh, that the same may be true of this message! While it is meant for one, and distinctly directed to his salvation, it may also, by the power of Jesus, save another not so clearly pointed at! While the Word is aimed at one particular character, may the Lord cause the very wind of the gospel to overcome another. While we spread the table for some bidden guest, may another hungry soul have grace given him to take his place at the banquet of grace! May those who hide away and whom, therefore, we are not likely to discover come forth to Jesus and touch Him and live!

This much-afflicted woman is important to understand for she is a typical character. While we describe her conduct and *her* cure, I trust she may serve as a looking glass in which many tremblers may see themselves. We shall fully note *what she had done* and then *what came of it.* This will lead us on to see *what she did at last* and *what we also should do.* May the Holy Spirit make this a very practical study by causing you to follow her till you gain the blessing as she did!

What She Had Done

The woman had been literally dying for twelve years. What had she been doing? Had she resigned herself to her fate or treated her malady as a small matter? Far from it. Her conduct is highly instructive.

First, *she had resolved not to die if a cure could be had.* She was evidently a woman of great determination and hopefulness. She knew that this disease of hers would cause her life to ebb away and bring her to the grave. But she said within herself, "I will fight against it. If there is a possibility of removing this plague, it shall be removed whatever the cost or pain." What a blessing it would be if unsaved ones would say each one for himself, "I am a lost soul, but if a lost soul can be saved, I will be saved. I am guilty, but if guilt can be washed away, mine shall be washed away. I have a hard heart, but if a heart of stone can be turned into a heart of flesh, I long to have it so. I will never rest until this gracious work is wrought in me!" Alas, it is not so with many! Indifference is the rule—indifference about their immortal souls! Many are sick with a deadly spiritual disease, but they make no resolve to have it cured. They trifle with sin and death, and heaven and hell.

Insensibility has seized upon many, and a proud conceit. They are full of sin, and yet they talk of self-righteousness. They are weak and can do nothing, yet they boast of their ability. They are not conscious of their true condition, and hence they have no desire to seek a cure. How should they desire healing when they do not believe that they are diseased? How sad that beneath the ruddy cheek of morality there should lurk the fatal illness of enmity to God! How horrible to be healthy on the outside and leprous within! Are there not many who can talk freely about religion and seem right with God, and yet in the secret of their hearts they are the victims of an insincerity and a lack of truth that fatally undermine the life of their profession. They are not what they seem to be. A secret sin drains away the lifeblood of their religion. May the Holy Spirit show us the fatal nature of our soul's disease, for this, I trust, would lead to the making of a firm resolve to find salvation, if salvation is to be had.

No doubt some are held back from such action by the freezing power of despair. They have reached the conclusion that there is no hope for them. The promises of the gospel they regard as the voice of God to others but as having no cheering word for them. One might suppose that they had searched the book of life and had made sure that their names were not written there. They act as if their death warrant had been signed. They cannot believe in the possibility of their becoming partakers of everlasting life. They are under a destroying delusion that leads them to abandon hope. None are more presumptuous than the despairing.

When men have no hope, they soon have no fear. Is not this a dreadful thing? May the Lord save you from such a condition! Despair of God's mercy is an unreasonable thing. If you think you have grounds for it, the lying spirit must have suggested them to you. Holy Scripture contains no justification for hopelessness. No mortal has a just pretense to perish in despair. Neither the nature of God nor the gospel of God nor the Christ of God warrants despair. Multitudes of texts encourage hope, but no one Scripture, rightly understood, permits a doubt of the mercy of God. "All manner of sin and blasphemy shall be forgiven unto men" (Matt. 12:31). Jesus, the great Healer, is never baffled by any disease of human nature. He can cast out a legion of devils and raise the dead. Oh, that I could whisper hope into the dull ear of those who mourn! Oh, that I could drop a rousing thought into the sullen heart of the self-condemned! How glad should I be! My poor desponding friend, I would fain see the chains snapped, your fetters broken off! Oh, that the Spirit of God would cause you, like this woman, to resolve that if there be healing for your soul, you will have it!

Alas! Many have never come to this gracious resolution, because they cherish a vain hope and are misled by an idle dream. They fancy that salvation will come to them without their seeking it. Certainly, they have no right to expect such a thing. It is true that our Lord is found of them that seek Him not, but that is an act of

His own sovereignty and is not a rule for our procedure. The plain directions of the gospel are. "Seek ye the LORD while he may be found, call ye upon him while he is near" (Isa. 55:6). How dare they set these gracious words aside? They fancy that they may wake up one of these fine days and find themselves saved. It may more likely happen to them as to the rich man in the parable: "In hell he lift up his eyes, being in torments" (Luke 16:23). God grant that you may not waste your soul in such misery!

Some fancy that at the time of death, they may cry, "God be merciful to me a sinner," and so may leap into salvation. It seems to them a very slight business to be reconciled to God. They imagine that they can be converted when they want, and so they put it off from day to day, as if it were of no more consequence than going to buy a coat. Believe me, the Word of God does not set forth the matter in this way. It tells us that even the righteous scarcely are saved, and it calls us to strive to enter in at the strait gate.

God save you from every false confidence that would prevent your being in earnest about the healing of your soul. Spiritually, your case is as desperate as that of the poor woman now before us. May the Lord sweetly constrain you to feel that you must be healed and that you cannot afford to put off the blessed day! If beneath the firmament of heaven there is healing for a sin-sick soul, seek it till you find it. When the Lord brings you to this resolve by His good Spirit, you will not be far from the kingdom of heaven.

Let us next note that *this woman, having made her resolve, adopted the best means she could think of.* Physicians are men set apart on purpose to deal with human maladies; therefore, she went to the physicians. What better could she do? Though she failed, yet she did what seemed most likely to succeed. Correspondingly, when a soul is resolved to find salvation, it is most right that it should use every available means for the finding of salvation. Oh, that they were wise enough to hear the gospel and to come at once to Jesus, but often they make grave mistakes. This woman went to those who were supposed to understand the science of medicine. Was it not natural that she should look to their superior wisdom for help?

Many in these days do the same thing spiritually. They hear of the new discoveries of professedly cultured men, hearing their talk about the littleness of sin and the nonnecessity of the new birth. Poor deceived creatures! They find in the long run that nothing comes of it, for the wisdom of man is nothing but pretentious folly. The world by wisdom knows neither God nor His salvation. Many people know all the less of saving truth because they know so much of what human fancy has devised and human search discovered. We cannot blame the woman who, being anxious for healing, went to those first who were thought to know most. But let us not, with Christ so near, go roundabout as she did, but let us touch our Lord at once.

No doubt the sufferer also tried men who were otherwise authorized to act as physicians. How can you blame her for going to those who had the official stamp? Many sin-sick souls nowadays are, at first, very hopeful that the ordained clergy can benefit them by their duly performed services and duly administered sacraments. At least, good men, eminent in the Church, may be looked to for aid; surely they should know how to deal with souls! Alas! It is vain to look to men at all and foolish to depend on official dignity or special repute. Some teachers do not know much about their own souls and therefore know less about the souls of others. Vain is the help of man, be the man who he may. Whatever his popularity, learning, or eloquence, if you seek him for his prayers or his teachings as being able to save you, you will certainly seek in vain, as this poor woman did. She is not to be blamed but is to be commended that she did what seemed best to her according to her light. But you are warned: go not, therefore, to men.

No doubt she met with some who boasted that they could heal her complaint at once. They began by saying, "You have tried So-and-so, but he is a mere quack. Mine is a scientific remedy. You have used a medicine that I could have told you would be worthless, but I have the secret. Put yourself absolutely into my hands, and the thing is done. I have healed many who had given up hope. Follow my orders, and you will be restored."

Sick persons are so eager to recover that they readily take the bait offered them by brazen impudence. An oily tongue and a bland manner, backed with unblushing assurance, are sure to win their way with one who is anxious to gain that which is offered. Ah, me! "All is not gold that glitters," and not all the professions that are made of helping sin-sick souls are true professions. Many are physicians of no value. There is no balm in Gilead. There is no physician there. If there had been, the hurt of the daughter of my people had long ago been healed. There is no medicine beneath the sky that can stop the tremblings of a heart that dreads the judgment to come. No earthly surgery can take away the load of sin from conscience. No hand of priest or presbyter, prophet or philosopher, can cleanse the leprosy of guilt. The finger of God is required here. There is one Heal-all, one divine *Catholicon*, and only one.

Happy is he who has received this infallible balm from Jehovah Rophi—the Lord that healeth (Ex. 15:26). Yet we marvel not that when souls are pressed down with a sense of guilt, they try anything and everything that offers even a faint hope of relief. I could wish that all my readers had an intense zeal to find salvation, for even if it led them into temporary mistakes, yet, under God's blessing, they would find their way out of them and end by glorifying the grace of our Lord Jesus Christ, which never fails.

This woman, in the next place, having resolved not to die if cure could be had and having adopted the best means, *persevered in the use of those means*. No doubt she tried many, and even opposite, remedies. One doctor said, "You had better go to the warm baths of the lake of Tiberias. Such bathing will be comforting and helpful." She grew worse at the warm baths and went to another physician, who said, "You were wrongly treated. You need the cold baths of the Jordan." Thus she went from vanity to vanity, only to find both of them useless. An eminent practitioner assured her that she needed an internal remedy and that he alone could give her an infallible medicine. This, however, was of no use to her, and she went to another, who said that an external application should be tried, such as Isaiah's lump of figs.

What perseverance that woman must have had! In those times, surgery was murderous and medicines were poisonous. Many of the prescriptions were sickening, and yet ridiculous. I read a prescription of our Savior's time, warranted to cure many diseases, that consisted of grasshopper eggs. The eggs were supposed to exercise a marvelous influence, but they are no longer on the list of medicines. The tooth of a fox was said to possess special powers. I noticed that one of the chief drugs of all, the most expensive but the surest in its action, was a nail from the finger of a man who had been hanged, but it required that the man should have been hanged. Poor creatures were made to suffer most painfully by cruel medicines that were far worse than the disease. As for surgical operations, if they had been designed to kill, they were certainly admirably arranged for their purpose. The wonder is that for twelve years the poor soul survived against the doctors. And the case is much the same spiritually. How many under their burden of sin go first to one and then to another. Practice this, agonize after that, and search for the other, perseveringly, and still without avail! Travel as fast as you may in a wrong direction, you will not reach the place you seek. Vain are all things save Jesus our Lord.

Have you been to Doctor Ceremony? He is at this time the popular doctor. Has he told you that you must attend to forms and rules? Has he prescribed you so many prayers and so many services. Ah! Many go to him, and they persevere in a round of religious observances, but these yield no lasting ease to the conscience. Have you tried Doctor Morality? He has a large practice and is a fine old Jewish physician. "Be good in outward character," says he, "and it will work inwardly and cleanse the heart." A great many persons are supposed to have been cured by him and by his assistance, Doctor Civility, who is nearly as clever as his master. But I have it on good evidence that neither of them apart, nor even the two together, could ever deal with an inward disease. Do what you may, your own doings will not heal the wounds of a bleeding heart. Doctor Mortification has also a select practice, but men are not saved by denying themselves until they first deny their self-righteousness. Doctor Excitement has many patients, but his cures seldom outlive the setting of the sun. Doctor Feeling is much sought after by tender spirits who try to feel sorrow and remorse, but indeed, the way of cure does not lie in that quarter. Let everything be done that can be done apart from our blessed Lord Jesus Christ, and the sick soul will be nothing bettered. You may try human remedies for the space of a lifetime, but sin will remain in power, guilt will cling to the conscience, and the heart will abide as hard as ever.

But *this woman also spent all her substance over it.* That was perhaps the chief thing in ancient surgery! This golden ointment that did good to the physician, whatever became of the patient. The most important point was to pay the doctor. This woman's living was wasting away as well as her life. She continued to pay and to pay and to pay, but she received no benefit from it all. Rather, she suffered more than she would have done had she kept her gold. Thus do men waste their thought, their care, their prayer, their agony over that which is as nothing. In the end there was an end to her means, but so long as the silver lasted, she lavished it out of the bag.

What would a man not give to be saved? I never am surprised that dying men give their estates to priests in the hope that they can save their souls. If gold could purchase pardon, who would withhold it? Health of body, if it could be purchased with gold, would be cheap at any price. But health of soul, holiness of character, acceptance with God, assurance of heaven—these would be cheap if we counted out worlds as poor men pay down their pennies for bread. There are men so mean that they would not part with a dollar for a place in Paradise, but if these once knew their true condition, they would alter their minds. The price of wisdom is above rubies. If we had mines of gold, we might profitably barter them for the salvation of our souls.

Beloved, you see where this woman was. She was in downright, desperate earnest to have her mortal malady healed, and so she spared neither her labor nor her living. In this we may wisely imitate her.

What Had Come of It

We are told that she had suffered many things of many physicians. That was her sole reward for trusting and spending: she had not been relieved, much less healed, but *she had suffered.* She had endured additional suffering through seeking a cure. That is the case with you who have not come to Christ but, being under a sense of sin, have sought relief apart from Him. All that you do apart from Jesus to win salvation will only cause you increased suffering. You may have tried to save yourself by prayers, but your prayers have turned your thoughts upon your sin and its punishment, and thus you have become more wretched than before. You have attended to ceremonies, and if you have used them sincerely, they have wrought in you a solemn sense of the holiness of God and of your own distance from Him. But this, though very proper, has only increased your sorrow. You have been trying to feel good and to do good so you may be good, but the very effort has made you feel how far off you are from the goodness you so desire. Your self-denial has excited cravings after evil, and your modifications have given new life to your pride. Efforts after salvation made in your own strength act like the struggles of a drowning man, who sinks the more surely. As the fruit of your desperate efforts, you have suffered all the more. In the end, I trust this may work for your good, but up till now it has served no healing purpose. When you are at death's door, all your praying, weeping, church going, and sacrament taking do not help you one bit.

There has been this peculiarly poignant pang about it all, that you are *nothing bettered*. Cheerily did you hope, but cruelly are you disappointed. You cried, "I have it this time," but the bubble vanished as you grasped it. The evil of your nature when repressed in one place broke out in another. You dealt with the symptoms of your disease, but you did not cut off the root of the mischief. It only showed itself in another form, but it never went away. You gave up one sin only to fall into another. You watched at the front entrance, and the thief stole in at the back door. Up till now, O soul, you have not come to Jesus, and after all your goings elsewhere, you are nothing bettered!

And now, perhaps, you are saying, "What can I do? What shall I do?" I will tell you. You can do nothing except what this woman ultimately did. You are now brought to this extremity—without strength, without merit, without power, you must look out of yourself to another, who has strength and merit and can save you. God grant that you may look to that glorious One now!

We read of this woman that though she suffered much, she was nothing better but *rather grew worse*. No better after twelve years of medicine? She went to one doctor after another and paid her remaining money, but she still went backward. She bought disappointment very dearly. Friend, is this your condition? You are anxious to be right, and, therefore, you are earnest in every effort to save yourself, but still you are nothing bettered. You climb a treadmill and are no higher after all your climbing. You drift down the river with one tide, and you float up again when it turns. Night after night you pull up in the same old creek that you started from. Oh, pitiful condition! Getting gray, too. Becoming quite the old gentleman, and yet no nearer eternal life than when, as a lad, you used to attend the house of God and wished to become a child of God.

Nothing bettered? No; she grew worse Other diseases fed upon her weakness, and she became more lifeless than ever. Sad result of so much perseverance! And is not that the case with some of you who are in earnest but are not enlightened? You are working and growing poorer as you work. There is not about you so much as there used to be of good feeling, or sincere desire, or prayerfulness, or love for the Bible, or care to hear the gospel. You are becoming more careless, more dubious than you once were. You have lost much of your former sensitiveness. You are doing certain things now that would have startled you years ago, and you are leaving certain matters undone that once you would have thought essential. Evidently you are caught in the current and are nearing the waterfalls. The Lord deliver you!

This is a sad, sad case! As a climax of it all, the heroine of our story had now *spent all that she had*. She could not go now to the doctors. She must do without their flattering speech in the future. As for those famous medicines that raised her hopes, she can buy no more of such costly inventions. This was, perhaps, her bitterest grief. But let me whisper it in your ear—this was the best thing that had yet happened to her, and I am praying that it may happen to some of you. At the bottom of your purse I trust you will find wisdom. When we come to the end of self, we come to the beginning of Christ. That last shekel binds us to the pretenders, but absolute bankruptcy sets us free to go to Him who heals diseases without money and without price. Glad enough am I when I meet with a man who is starved out of self-sufficiency. Welcome! Now you are ready for Jesus. When all your own virtue has gone out of you, then shall you seek and find the virtue that flows from Him.

What This Woman Did At Last

Weaker and weaker had she become, and her purse had become lighter and lighter. She hears of Jesus of Nazareth, a man sent of God who is healing sick folk of all sorts. She listens attentively, puts the stories together that she hears, then believes them. They have the sound of truth about them. "Oh," she says, "there is yet another opportunity for me. I will get in the crowd, and if I can only touch the border of his garment, I shall be made whole." Splendid faith! It was thought much of in her own day, and we may still more highly prize it now that faith has grown so rare.

Note well *she resolved to trust in Jesus in sheer despair of doing anything else*. My dear friend, I wish I might come up to you and say to you personally, "Try Jesus Christ, trust Him, and see whether He will not save you. Every other door is evidently shut. Why not enter by Christ the door?" There is no other lifebuoy. Lay hold on this! Exercise the courage that is born of desperation. May God the Holy Spirit help you to thrust forth your finger and get into touch with Jesus! Say, "Yes, I freely accept Christ. By God's grace, I will have Him to be my only hope. I will have Him now." Be driven to Jesus by force of circumstances. Since there is no other port, O weatherbeaten vessel, make for this one! Wanderer, here is a refuge! Turn in hither, for there is no other shelter.

After all, *this was the simplest and easiest thing that she could do*. Touch Jesus. Put out your finger and touch the hem of His garment. The prescriptions she had purchased were long, but this was short enough. The operations performed upon her had been intricate, but this was simplicity itself. The suffering she had endured had complicated her case, but this was as plain as a stick. "Touch with your finger the hem of His garment: that is all." You may have tried many things, great things, and hard things, and painful things. Why not try this simple matter of faith? Believe in the Lord Jesus Christ, and you will be saved. Trust Jesus to cleanse you, and He will do it. Put yourself into your Savior's hands once for all, and He will save you.

Not only was this the simplest and easiest thing for the poor afflicted one, but certainly *it was the freest and most gracious*. There was not a penny to pay. Nobody stood at the door of the consulting room to take her money. The good Physician did not even give a hint that He expected a reward. The gifts of Jesus are free as the air. He healed this believing woman in the open street, in the midst of the crowd. She had felt that if she could but get into the throng, she would, by hook or by crook, get near enough to reach the hem of His garment, and then she would be healed. It is so even now. Come and receive grace freely. Bring no good works, no good words, no good feelings, no good resolves, as the price of pardon. Come with an empty hand and touch the Lord by faith. The good things that you desire, Jesus will give you as the result of His cure, but they cannot be the cause or the price of it. Accept His mercy as the gift of His love! Come empty-handed and receive! Come undeserving and be favored! Only come into contact with Jesus, who is the fountain of life and health, and you shall be saved.

This was the quietest thing for her to do. She said nothing. She did not cry aloud like the blind men. She did not ask friends to look on and watch her make her venture. She kept her own counsel and pushed into the press. In absolute silence, she took a stolen touch of the Lord's robe. And so can you be saved in silence. You have no need to speak to any person of your acquaintance, not even to mother or father. At this moment, believe and live. Nobody will know that you now are touching the Lord. In later days you will own your faith, but in the act itself you will be alone and unseen. Believe on Jesus. Trust yourself with Him. Have done with all other confidences and say, "He is all my salvation." Take Jesus at once, if not with a hand's grasp, yet with a finger's touch. O poor, timid, bashful creature, touch the Lord! Trust in His power to save. Do not let me tell you to do it in vain, but do it at once. May God's Spirit cause you to accept Jesus now!

This is *the only effectual thing.* Touch Jesus, and salvation is yours at once. Simple as faith is, it is never failing. A touch of the fringe of the Savior's garment sufficed. In a moment she felt in her body that she was healed of that plague. "It is twelve years ago," she said to herself, "since I felt like a living woman. I have been sinking in a constant death all this while, but now I feel my strength come back to me." Blessed be the name of the great Healer! She was exceedingly glad. Tremble she did, lest it should turn out to be too good to be true. But she was most surely healed. Do trust my Lord, for He will surely do for you that which none other can achieve. Leave feeling and working, and try faith in Jesus. May the Holy Spirit lead you to do so at once!

Do As This Woman Did

Ask nobody about it, but do it. She did not go to Peter, James, and John and say, "Good sirs, advise me." She did not beg from them an introduction to Jesus, but she went of her own accord and tried for herself the virtue of a touch. You have had advising enough; now come to real work. There is too much tendency to console ourselves by conversations with godly men. Let us get away from them and speak to their Master. Talks and chats are all very well, but one touch of Jesus will be infinitely better. Press on till, by personal faith, you have laid hold on Jesus. Do not tell anybody what you are about to do; wait till it is done. Another day you will be happy to tell the minister and God's people of what the Lord has done for you; but for the present, quietly believe in the Lamb of God who takes away the sin of the world.

Do not even ask yourself about it. If this poor woman had consulted with herself, she might never have ventured so near the Holy One of God. So clearly shut out from society by the law of her people and her God, if she had given the matter a second thought, she might have abandoned the idea. Blessed was the impetuosity that thrust her into the crowd and kept her head above the throng and her face toward the Lord in the center of the crowd. She did not so much reason as dare. Do not ask yourself anything about it, but do it. Believe, and have done with it. Stop not to argue with your own unbelief or answer your rising doubts and fears, but at once, upon the instant, put out your finger, touch the hem of His garment, and seek what will come of it.

Yield to the sacred impulse that is just now operating upon you. Do not say, "Tomorrow may be more convenient." In this woman's case, there was the Lord before her. She longed to be healed at once, and so, come what may, into the crowd she plunged. One wonders how she managed to get near Him, but there was her chance, and she seized it. There was the fringe of the Lord's mantle; out went her finger: it was all done. O my friend, you have an opportunity now for God's great grace. Jesus of

Nazareth passes by at this moment. Oh, how I wish I could lead you to that saving touch! The Spirit of God can do it. May He now move you to cry, "I will believe and trust my soul with Jesus!" Have you done so? You are saved. "He that believeth on the Son hath everlasting life" (John 3:36).

"Oh, but I tremble so!" Her hand shook, but she touched Him all the same for that. I think I see her quivering finger. Poor woman, with pale and bloodless cheeks! What a taper finger was that which she held out, and how it quivered! However much the finger of your faith may tremble, if it does but touch the hem of the Lord's garment, virtue will flow from Him to you. The power is not in the finger that touches but in the divine Savior who is touched. So long as there is a contact established between you and the almighty power of Jesus, His power will travel along your trembling finger and bring healing to your heart. A wire may skate with the wind and yet convey the electric current, and so may a trembling faith convey salvation from Jesus. A strong faith that rests anywhere but in Jesus is a delusion, but a weak faith that rests alone on Jesus, brings sure salvation. Out with your finger! Dear soul, out with your finger! Do not stop till you have touched the Lord by a believing prayer or hope. By the living God, I do implore you, trust the living Redeemer. As I shall meet you, face to face, before the judgment seat of Christ, I do implore and beseech you, put out the finger of faith and trust the Lord Jesus, who is so fully worthy to be trusted. The simple trust of your heart will stay the death that now works in you. Lord, give that trust, for Jesus' sake!

*L*earn a simple lesson from this man, I pray you. He made use of what senses he had. He could hear, if he could not see. We have heard people talk about their natural inability to perform gracious acts, and we have not answered them, because it will be time enough to talk of what they cannot do when they have done what they can do. There are some things that we are sure they can do, and these they have neglected. It is mere hypocrisy, therefore, for them to be pleading want of power when they do not use the strength they have. They do not constantly hear the gospel, or, if they do, they do not listen with attention, and, consequently, they do not get faith, for "faith cometh by hearing" (Rom. 10:17). In the case of Bartimaeus, everything was honest and sincere. The man had no eyes, but he had ears and a tongue, and he took care to use the faculties that remained to him so that when the Savior passed by, he cried to Him with all his might. He made his confession of faith and offered at the same time a personal petition for mercy as he cried aloud, "Thou Son of David, have mercy on me."

Chapter Seven

Good Cheer from
Christ's Call and from Himself

And they came to Jericho: and as he went out of Jericho with his disciples and a great number of people, blind Bartimaeus, the son of Timaeus, sat by the highway side begging. And when he heard that it was Jesus of Nazareth, he began to cry out, and say, Jesus, thou son of David, have mercy on me. And many charged him that he should hold his peace: but he cried the more a great deal, Thou Son of David, have mercy on me. And Jesus stood still, and commanded him to be called. And they call the blind man, saying unto him, Be of good comfort, rise; he calleth thee. And he, casting away his garment, rose, and came to Jesus. And Jesus answered and said unto him, What wilt thou that I should do unto thee? The blind man said unto him, Lord, that I might receive my sight. And Jesus said unto him, Go thy way; thy faith hath made thee whole. And immediately he received his sight, and followed Jesus in the way—Mark 10:46–52.

THE BLIND MAN DESCRIBED in this narrative is a picture of what I earnestly desire that every reader may become. In his first condition, Bartimaeus was a type of what the sinner is by nature—blind, hopelessly blind, unless the healing Savior shall interfere and pour in upon him the light of day. It is not, however, to this point that we shall now turn our thoughts but to his conduct while seeking sight. This man, by God's great mercy, so acted that he may be held up as an example to all who feel their spiritual blindness and earnestly desire to see the light of grace.

Several of the blind men of Scripture are very interesting individuals. There was one of them—the man born blind—who baffled the Pharisees by answering them with cool courage mixed with shrewdness and mother wit (John 9). Well might his parents say that he was of age, for he had all his wits about him. Blind as he had been, he could see a great deal; and when his eyes were opened, he proved beyond all dispute that his questioners deserved the name of "Blind Pharisees" that the Lord Jesus gave them.

Bartimaeus, the son of Timaeus, is another notable character. There is a sharp-cut individuality and crispness of style about him that makes him a remarkable person. He is one who thinks and acts for himself, is not soon daunted or easily swayed, makes sure of what he knows, and when he is questioned gives a clear reply. I suppose that as he sat in the midnight darkness that was his perpetual state, he thought much, and having heard that from the seed of David there had arisen a great prophet who worked miracles and preached glad tidings to the poor, he studied the matter over and concluded that His claims were true. A blind man might well see that fact, if at all familiar with Old Testament prophecy. And as he heard more and more of Jesus and compared Him with the prophetic description of the coming King, he felt convinced that Jesus was the promised Messiah. Then, he thought within himself, "If He were ever to come this way, I would announce myself as one of His followers. I would proclaim Him King, whether others acknowledge His royalty or not. I would act as a herald to the great Prince and shout aloud that He is the Son of David." Then he further resolved to seek the pity of the Messiah and beg for his sight, for it was foretold that the Messiah would come to open blind eyes (Isa. 35:5). This resolution he had so long dwelt upon that when the time did come and he heard that Jesus passed by, he immediately availed himself of the opportunity and cried out with all his might, "Thou Son of David, have mercy on me." Oh, that you who read these lines would think over the claims of Jesus and come to the same conclusion as the blind beggar of Jericho!

Learn a simple lesson from this man, I pray you. He made use of what senses he had. He could *hear*, if he could not see. We have heard people talk about their natural inability to perform gracious acts, and we have not answered them, because it will be time enough to talk of what they cannot do when they have done what they can do. There are some things that we are sure they can do, and these they have neglected. It is mere hypocrisy, therefore, for them to be pleading want of power when they do not use the strength they have. They do not constantly hear the gospel, or, if they do, they do not listen with attention, and, consequently, they do not get faith, for "faith cometh by hearing" (Rom. 10:17). In the case of Bartimaeus, everything was honest and sincere. The man had no eyes, but he had ears and a tongue, and he took care to use the faculties that remained to him so that when the Savior passed by, he cried to Him with all his might. He made his confession of faith and offered at the same time a personal petition for mercy as he cried aloud, "Thou Son of David, have mercy on me."

I wish to drive at one point only, which will stand out clearly when I have finished. But I must go a little roundabout to accomplish my design. May the Holy Spirit dictate every word!

He Sought the Lord Under Great Discouragements

He cried to the Lord Jesus so loudly, so unceremoniously, and at so unseasonable a time, as others thought, that they tried to stop him. But this was like pouring gasoline upon a fire, and it only made him the more intense in his pleading.

Notice his first discouragement: *no one prompted him to cry to Christ*. No friend lovingly whispered in his ears, "Jesus of Nazareth passes by. Now is your opportunity to seek His face!" Possibly you have been so neglected that you have sighed, "No one cares for my soul." Then yours is a parallel case to that of Bartimaeus. Very few can honestly make this complaint if they live among lively Christians for, in all probability, they have often been invited, entreated, and almost compelled to come to Christ. Some even complain of Christian witnessing and are weary of it, not liking to be spoken to about their souls. "Intrusion" it has been called by some cavillers, but indeed it is a blessed intrusion upon a sinner, slumbering in his sin over the brink of hell, to disturb his slumbers and arouse him to flee for his life. Would you not think it ridiculous, were a house on fire, if the fireman declined to fetch anybody out of the house because he had not been introduced to the family? I reckon that a breach of courtesy is often a most courteous thing when the desire is the benefit of an immortal soul. If I say a very personal thing and it arouses anyone to seek and find salvation, I know that he will never blame me on that score.

Still, a person may reside where there is no one to invite him to seek Jesus, and if so, he may recall the example of this man, who, all unprompted, sought the Savior's aid. He knew his need without being told. And believing that Jesus could give him his eyesight, he did not need convincing to pray to Him. He thought for himself, as all should do. Will not you do the same, especially on a matter so weighty as the salvation of your own soul? What if you have never been the subject of friendly entreaties, yet you should not require them. You are possessed of your reason. You know that you are already sinful and will be lost forever unless the Lord Jesus saves you. Does not common sense suggest that you should cry to Him at once? Be at least as sensible as this poor blind beggar, and let the voice of your earnest prayer go up to Jesus, the Son of David.

The discouragement of Bartimaeus was still greater, for when he did begin to cry, *those around discouraged him.* Read the 48th verse: "*Many* charged him that he should hold his peace." Some for one reason, and some for another, charged him that he should be quiet. They did not merely advise him, but they "*charged* him." They spoke like people in authority. "Be quiet, will you? Be still! What are you at!" Judging him to be guilty of a grave impropriety in disturbing the eloquence of the great Preacher, they would have hushed him to silence. Those who do not suffer under a sense of sin often think awakened sinners are out of order and fanatical when they are only in earnest. The people near the blind beggar blamed him for his bad taste in shouting so loudly, "Thou Son of David, have mercy on me."

But he was not to be stopped. On the contrary, we are told that "*he cried the more,*" and not only the more but also "the more *a great deal,*" so that it was time wasted to try to silence him. One man thought that surely he would put him down and therefore spoke most authoratively, but he gained nothing by the effort, for the blind man shouted still more lustily, "Thou Son of David, have mercy on me." Here was an opportunity for having his eyes opened, and he would not miss it to please anybody. Folks around him might misjudge him, but that would not matter if Jesus opened his eyes. Sight was the one thing needful, and for that he could put up with rebuffs and reproaches. To him, discouragements were encouragements, and when they said, "Be silent," he cried the more a great deal. His manhood and determination were developed by opposition.

Friend, how is it with you? Can you defy the opinion of ungodly men and dare to be singular that you may be saved? Can you brave opposition and discouragement, resolving that if mercy is to be had, you will have it? Opposers will call your determination obstinacy, but never mind; your firmness is the stuff of which martyrs are made. In a wrong cause, a strong will creates incorrigible rebels. But if it is sanctified, it gives great force to character and steadfastness to faith. Bartimaeus must have sight, and he will have sight, and there is no stopping him. He is blind to all hindrances and pushes through. He had been begging so long that he knew how to beg importunately. He was as sturdy a beggar with Christ as he had been with men, and so he followed up his suit in the teeth of all who would stave him off.

There was, however, one more discouragement that must have weighed on him far more than the want of prompting and the presence of opposition: *Jesus himself did not answer him at first.* He had evidently, according to the run of the narrative, cried out to Jesus many times, for how else could it be said, "He cried the more a great deal"? His cry had risen stronger and stronger, but yet there was no reply. What was worse, the Master had been moving on. We are sure of that because we are told in the forty-ninth verse that Jesus, at length, "stood still," implying that before this time, He had been walking along, speaking as He went to the crowd around Him. Jesus was passing away—passing away without granting his desire, without giving a sign of having heard him.

Are you one who has cried for mercy long and found it not? Have you been praying for a month, and is there no answer? Is it longer still? Have you spent weary days and nights in waiting and watching for mercy? There is a mistake at the bottom of the whole affair that I will not explain just now, but I will tell you how to act. Even if Jesus does not appear to hear you, be not discouraged but cry to Him "the more a great deal." Remember, He loves importunity, and sometimes He waits awhile on purpose that our prayers may gather strength and that we may be the more earnest. Cry to Him, dear heart. Be not desponding. Do not give up in despair. Mercy's gate has oiled hinges, and it swings easily; push at it again. If you will use the knocker long enough, the porter will open to you and say, "Come in, thou blessed of the Lord. Why do you stand without?" Have the courage of this poor blind man and say, "Though for a while He may not hear me, yet still will I confess Him to be the son of David and so avow that He is able to save me, and still will I cry to Him, 'Thou Son of David, have mercy on me.'"

Note, then, that this blind man is an example to us because he did not take much notice of discouragements, whatever they were. He had within himself a spring of action that none could dry up. He was resolved to draw near to the great Physician and put his case into His hands. O my dear friend, let this be your firm determination, and you too shall yet be saved.

After Awhile, He Received Encouragement

"Jesus stood still, and commanded him to be called." The encouragement was given to him not by our Lord but by the same persons who had formerly rebuked him. Christ did not say to him, "Be of good comfort," because the man was not in need of such a word. The man was by no means backward or disconsolate or staggered by the opposition he had met with. Jesus Christ said, "Be of good cheer," in the case of the poor paralytic man who was let down by cords from the roof because he was sad at heart. But this man was already of good courage, and therefore the Savior gave him no superfluous consolation. The onlookers were pleased with the hope of seeing a miracle and so offered their encouragements, which were not of any great worth or weight, since they came from lips that a few minutes before had been singing quite another tune.

At this point, I wish to give to all anxious souls who are trying to find their Savior some little word of cheer, and yet I warn them not to think too much of it, for they need something far better than anything that man can say. The comfort given to Bartimaeus was drawn from the fact that Christ called him. "Be of good comfort, rise; *he calleth thee.*" To every sinner who is anxious to find Jesus, this is a note from the silver trumpet. You are invited to Jesus and need not therefore be afraid to come. In one sense or another, it is true of all who hear the gospel, "He calleth thee," and therefore to every one of our hearers we may say, "Be of good cheer."

First, it is true that Jesus calls each of us by *the universal call of the gospel*, for its message is for all people. Ministers are told to go into all the world and preach the gospel to every creature. You, my friend, are a creature, and consequently, the gospel has a call for you: "Believe on the Lord Jesus Christ, and thou shalt be saved" (Acts 16:31). We are commanded to preach the gospel of the kingdom throughout all nations and to cry, "Whosoever will, let him take the water of life freely" (Rev. 22:17). "Whosoever." There is no limit to it, and it would be a violation of our commission if we should attempt to enclose what God has made as free as the air and as universal as manhood. "The times of this ignorance God winked at; but now commandeth all men every where to repent" (Acts 17:30). This is the universal call: "Repent ye, and believe the gospel" (Mark 1:15). In this there is comfort of hope for all who desire to come to God.

But there is still more comfort in what, for distinction's sake, we will name *the character call*. Many promises in the Word of God are directed to persons of a certain character. For instance, "Come unto me, all ye that labour and are heavy laden, and I will give you rest" (Matt. 11:28). Do you labor? Are you heavy laden? Then Christ specially calls you and promises rest *to you* if you come to Him. Here is another: "Ho, every one that thirsteth, come ye to the waters" (Isa. 55:1). Are you thirsting after something better than this world can give? Then the Lord bids you come to the waters of His grace. "And he that hath no money; come ye" (Isa. 55:1). Is that you? Are you destitute of merit—destitute of everything that could purchase the favor of God? Then you are the person whom He specially invites. We find a very large number of invitations, both in the Old and New Testaments, addressed to persons in certain conditions and positions. When we meet with a person whose case is thus anticipated, we are bound to bid him be of good cheer, because the Lord is plainly calling him.

Next, there is *a ministerial call*, which is made useful to many. At times, the Lord enables His servants to give calls to people in a very remarkable way. They describe the case so accurately, even to the little touches, that the hearer says, "Somebody must have told the preacher about me." When personal and pointed words are thus put into our mouths by the Holy Spirit, we may give our hearer comfort and say, "Arise, he calleth *thee*." What did the woman of Samaria say? "Come, see a man, which told me all things that ever I did: is not this the Christ?" (John 4:29). When your inmost secrets are revealed—when the Word of God enters you as the priest's keen knife opened the sacrificial victim, laying bare your inward and secret thoughts and intents, you may say, "Now have I felt the power of that Word, which is quick and powerful. Oh, that I might also know its healing power!" When a call to repentance and faith comes on the back of a minute personal description, you may assuredly gather that the Lord has sent this message especially to you, and it is your right and privilege at once to feel the comfort of the fact that Jesus calls *you*: "To you is the word of this salvation sent" (Acts 13:26).

Yet there is another call that overtops these three, for the universal call and the character call and the ministerial call are none of them effectual to salvation unless they are attended with the Holy Ghost's own personal and *effectual call*. His call is known when you feel within yourself a secret drawing to Christ that you do not understand yet cannot resist. When you experience a tenderness of spirit, a softness of heart toward the Lord. When your soul kindles with a hope to which it was previously a stranger and your heart begins to sigh and almost to sing at the same time for love of God. When the Spirit of God brings Jesus near you and brings you near to Jesus. Then we may apply to you this message: "Be of good comfort, rise; he calleth thee."

He Overleaped Both Discouragement and Encouragement and Came to Jesus Himself

Bartimaeus did not care one whit more for the comfort than he did for the rebuffs of those around him. This is a point to be well observed. You who are seeking Jesus must not rest in *our* encouragements but must press on to Jesus. We would cheer you, but we hope you will not be satisfied with our cheering. Do what this blind man did. Let us read the text again: "Jesus stood still, and commanded him to be called. And they call the blind man, saying unto him, Be of good comfort, rise; he calleth thee. And he, casting away his garment, rose, and came to Jesus." He did not give them a "thank you" for their comfort. He did not stop half a minute to accept or to reject it. He did not need it: he wanted Christ, and nothing else.

Dear friend, whenever any man, with the best intentions in the world, tries to comfort you before you believe in Jesus, I hope you will pass him by and press on to the Lord himself. All comfort short of Christ himself is perilous comfort. You must come at once to Christ. You must hasten personally to Jesus and have your eyes opened by Him. You must not be comforted till He comforts you by working a miracle of grace. I fear we pamper you too much in unbelief, applying balm that does not come from the mountain of myrrh or from the sacrifice of our redeeming Lord. I fear that we talk as if there were balm in Gilead, but there is none anywhere except at Calvary. If there is a balm in Gilead, the Lord inquires, "Why then is not the health of the daughter of My people recovered?" The ointment of Comfort-apart-from-Christ has been tried long enough and has healed none. It is high time to point you to Christ Jesus Himself. Even the consolation to be drawn from the face of a man's being called requires much caution in its use lest we do mischief with it. The true eye salve is with Jesus himself. Unless the soul comes actually into personal contact with Christ, no other comforts should satisfy it, for they cannot save. Note with admiration, then, that this man did not content himself with the best comforts that friendly lips could utter, but he was eager to reach the Son of David.

We read first that *he arose*. He had been sitting down before, wrapped up in his great cloak in which he had often sat begging. Now that he heard that he was called, he, according to some versions, "leaped to his feet." The expression may be, perhaps, too strong, but at least he rose up eagerly and was no laggard. His opportunity had come, and he was ready for it, nay, hungering for the chance. Now, dear friend, I pray you, let neither discouragements nor comforts keep you sitting still, but rise with eagerness. Be stirred up to seek the Lord! Let all that is within you be aroused to come unto the Savior.

The blind man was on his feet in far less time than it takes to tell, and as he rose, *he flung off his old cloak* that might have hindered him. He did not care what he left or lost so long as he found his sight. His mantle had, no doubt, been very precious to him many times when he was a poor beggar. But now that he wanted to get to Jesus, he flung it away as if it were worth nothing, so that he might get through the throng more quickly and reach the One in whom his hopes centered. So, then, if anything impedes you in coming to your Savior, fling it off. God help you to be rid of self and sin and everything that is in the way. If any bad company you have been accustomed to keep, if any bad habit into which you have fallen, if anything dear as life hinders you from simple faith in Jesus, regard it as an evil to be renounced. Off with it, and make a rush to Him who calls you. Now, even now, draw near, and cast yourself at the Redeemer's feet. Say within yourself, "Encouraged or discouraged, I have weighed the matter, and I perceive that faith in Christ will save me. Jesus Christ will give me peace and rest, and I mean to have Him at once, whoever hinders or helps."

Then we are told that *he came to Jesus*. He did not stop halfway, but emboldened by Christ's call, he came right up to Him. He did not stay with Peter, or James, or John, or any of them, but he came to Jesus. Oh, that you, my friend, may have faith in Jesus Christ and trust in Him at once, putting your case by a distinct and personal act into Jesus Christ's hands that He may save you!

Our Lord was well aware that this man knew His name and character, and so, without giving him further instruction, Jesus addressed him in these words: "What wilt thou that I should do unto thee?" Our Lord's addresses to people were usually based upon their condition. Jesus knew that this man very clearly understood what he wanted, and so He put the question that he might openly give the answer. "What wilt thou that I should do unto thee?" "Lord," said he, "that I might look up," or, as our version has it, "that I might receive my sight."

Go, dear friend, to Jesus, whether comforted or discouraged, and tell Him what ails you. Describe your case in plain words. Do not say, "I cannot pray. I cannot find language." Any language will do if it is sincere. In the matter of speech, Jesus does not want hyacinths from a conservatory. He is delighted with field flowers plucked from any hedge where you can find them. Give to Him such words as come first to hand when your desires are fully awake. Tell Him you are a wretch undone without His sovereign grace. Tell Him you are a sinner worthy of death. Tell Him you have a hard heart. Tell Him all of your heart, as the Samaritan woman did of whom we read in the gospel. Then tell Him that you need forgiveness and a new heart. Speak out your soul, and hide nothing. Out with it! Out with it! Do not stay listening to sermons or consulting with Christian friends, but go and speak with Jesus. This will do you good. May the Divine Spirit lead you to do this *now* if you have never accepted Jesus before.

When Bartimaeus had stated his case in faith, he received more than he had asked for. He received salvation—so the word may be rendered.

He was made whole, and so saved. Whatever had caused his blindness was entirely taken away. He had his sight, and he could look up, a saved man. Do you believe that Jesus Christ is as able to save souls as He was to heal bodies? Do you believe that in His glory He is as able to save now as He was when He was a humble man here below? If there is any difference, He must have much more power than He had then. Do you believe that He is the same loving Savior now as He was when here on earth? O soul, I pray you to argue this out with yourself and say, "I will go to Jesus immediately. I never find that He cast out any. Why should He cast out me? No bodily disease baffled Him, and He is Master of the soul as well as of the body. Why should my soul disease baffle Him? I will trust Him and see whether He will save me or not. Discouraged or encouraged, I leave others behind, and I will go to the Savior." That is the lesson that I would have every unsaved soul learn. I would have him go beyond the outward means of grace to the secret fountain of grace, even to the great sacrifice for sin. Go to the Savior Himself, whether others cheer you or frown upon you. Dejected, rejected, neglected, yet come to Jesus and learn that you are elected to be perfected in Him.

One thing more about Bartimaeus. I want this man to be an example to all of us if we get a blessing from our Lord and are saved. *Having found Christ, he stuck to Him.* Jesus said to him, "Go thy way." Did he go his way? Yes, but what way did he choose? Read the last sentence: "He followed Jesus in the way." The way of Jesus was *his* way. He in effect said, "Lord, I do go my way when I follow You. I can now see for myself and can therefore choose my way, and I make this my first and last choice, that I will follow You in every pathway You mark out."

Oh, that everyone who professes to have received Christ would actually follow Him! But, alas, many are like those nine lepers who received healing for their bodies, but only one of them returned to praise Jesus. Great numbers, after revival services, are like the nine lepers; they declare that they are saved, but they do not live to glorify God. How is this? "Were there not ten cleansed?" (Luke 17:17). In great disappointment we inquire, "Where are the nine?" Alas, we ask with bleeding hearts, "Where are the nine?" They are not steadfast in our doctrine and fellowship or in breaking of bread. They are neither active in service nor exemplary in character. Where are they? Where? Echo answers, "Where?" But this man was of a nobler breed. When he received his sight, he "followed Jesus in the way."

He used his sight for the best of purposes; he saw his Lord and kept to His company. He determined that He who gave him his eyes should have his eyes. He could never see a more delightful sight than the Son of David who had removed his blindness, and so he stayed with Him that he might feast his eyes upon Him. If God has given your soul peace and joy and liberty, use your new-found liberty in delighting yourself in His dear Son.

Bartimaeus became Christ's avowed disciple. He had already proclaimed Him as the royal Son of David, and now he determines to be one of David's band. He enlists under the Son of David and marches with Him to the conflict at Jerusalem. He stayed with our great David in the hold, to share His persecutions and to go with Him to death itself. We are told that he went with Jesus in the way, and that way was up to Jerusalem, where his Leader was soon to be spit upon and to be mocked and to be crucified. Bartimaeus followed a despised and crucified Christ. Friend, will you do the same? Will you fare as he fared and endure reproach for His sake? Brave men are wanted for these evil times. We have too many of those thin-skinned professors who faint if society gives them the cold shoulder. Power to walk with a crucified Lord into the very jaws of the lion is a glorious gift of the Holy Ghost. May it rest on you, dear friend, to a full degree! May the Spirit of God help you!

This Bartimaeus, the son of Timaeus, is a fine man. When he is once really aroused, you can see that he possesses a firm, decided, noble manhood. Many nowadays bend to every breeze, like the willow by the stream, but this man held his own. Most men are made of soft material that will run into every mold, but this man had stern stuff within him. When he was a blind man, he cried till he received his sight, though Peter and James and John forbade him. And when he became a seeing man, he followed Jesus at all costs, though shame and spitting lay before him. It is our impression that he remained a steadfast and well-known disciple of Jesus, for Mark, who is the most graphic of all the gospel writers, always means much by every stroke of his pen. Mark mentions him as Bartimaeus, whose name signifies "son of Timaeus," and then he further explains that his name really has that meaning. A name may not be actually correct, for many a Johnson is not the son of John, many a Williamson is not the son of William, and so there might possibly have been a Bartimaeus who was not the son of Timaeus. Mark, however, writes as if Timaeus were very well known, and his son was known, too. The father was probably a poor believer known to all the Church, and the son made his mark in the Christian community. I should not wonder whether he was what we call "a character" in the Church, known to everybody for his marked individuality and force of mind.

If, my friend, you have been long in seeking salvation and have become discouraged, may the Lord give you resolution to come to Jesus Christ this very day. Bring that firm, steadfast mind of yours and bow it to Jesus, and He will accept you and end your darkness. Under His teaching you may yet become a marked man in the

Church, of whom in later years believers will say, "You know that man—that grievous sinner while he was unsaved, that eager seeker when he was craving mercy, that earnest worker after he became a believer: he will not be put back by anybody. He is a true man who gives his whole heart to our Lord." I shall be delighted beyond measure if you should be such a convert—a man who will not need looking after, but a determined man, resolute to do right, cost what it may. Such persons are a great gain to the good cause. Gently would I whisper to you, *Will not you be one of them?*

*H*ear me, O trembling sinner: if you are as full of sin as an egg is full of meat, Jesus can remove it all. If your propensities to sin are as untameable as the wild boar of the wood, yet Jesus Christ, the Lord of all, can subdue your iniquities and make you the obedient servant of His love. Jesus can turn the lion into a lamb, and He can do it now. He can transform you where you are sitting, saving you while you read this word. All things are possible to the Savior God, and all things are possible to him who believes. I would you had such a faith as this leper had, although if it were even less, it might be enough, since you have not all his difficulties to contend with, because Jesus has already saved many sinners like yourself and changed many hearts as hard as yours. If He shall regenerate you, He will be doing for you no strange thing but only one of the daily miracles of His grace. He has now healed thousands of your fellow lepers. Can you not believe that He can heal the leprosy in you?

Chapter Eight

The Lord and the Leper

And there came a leper to him, beseeching him, and kneeling down to him, and saying unto him, If thou wilt, thou canst make me clean. And Jesus, moved with compassion, put forth his hand, and touched him, and saith unto him, I will; be thou clean. And as soon as he had spoken, immediately the leprosy departed from him, and he was cleansed—Mark 1:40–42.

IN THE VERSES PRECEDING our text, we see that our Lord had been engaged in special prayer. He had gone alone on the mountainside to have communion with God. Simon and the rest search for Him, and He comes away in the early morning with the burrs from the hillside upon His garments, the smell of the field upon Him, even of a field that the Lord God had blessed. Jesus comes forth among the people, charged with power that He had received in communion with the Father, and now we may expect to see wonders. And we do see them, for devils fear and fly when He speaks the Word. Finally, there comes to Him one, an extraordinary being, condemned to live apart from the rest of men lest he should spread defilement all around. A leper comes and kneels before Him, expressing his confident faith in Him, that Jesus can make him whole. Now is the Son of Man glorious in His power to save.

The Lord Jesus Christ at this day has all power in heaven and in earth. He is charged with a divine energy to bless all who come to Him for healing. Oh, that we may see today some great wonder of His power and grace! Oh, for one of the days of the Son of Man here and now! To that end it is absolutely needful that we should find a case for His spiritual power to work upon. Is there not one reader in whom His grace may prove its omnipotence? Not you who are self-righteous! You yield Him no space to work in. You who are whole have no need of a physician (Matt. 9:12). In you there is no opportunity for Jesus to display His miraculous force.

Yonder are the ones we seek. Forlorn and lost, full of evil and self-condemned, you are the characters we seek. You who feel as if you were possessed with evil spirits, and you who are leprous with sin, you are the persons in whom Jesus will find ample room for the display of His holy skill. Of you I might say, as Jesus once said of the man born blind: you are here that the works of God may be manifest in you (John 9:3). With your guilt and your depravity, you furnish the empty vessels into which His grace may be poured, the sick souls upon whom He may display His matchless power to bless and save. Be hopeful, then. Look up for the Lord's approach and expect that even in you He will work great marvels. This leper shall be a picture—I hope a mirror—in whom you will see yourself. I do pray that as I go over the details of this miracle many may put themselves in the leper's place and do just as the leper did, receiving a cleansing from the hand of Christ. O Spirit of the living God, I ask You to work, that Jesus, the Son of God, may be glorified here and now!

This Leper's Faith Made Him Eager to Be Healed

He was a leper. I will not stay just now to describe what horrors are compacted into that single word. But he believed that Jesus could cleanse him, and his belief stirred him to an anxious desire to be healed at once.

Alas, we have to deal with spiritual lepers eaten up with the foul disease of sin! But *some of them do not believe that they ever can be healed*, and the consequence is that despair makes them sin most greedily. "I may as well be hanged for a sheep as for a lamb," is the inward impression of many a sinner when he fears that there is no mercy and no help for him. Because they have no hope, they plunge deeper and yet deeper into the slough of iniquity. Oh, that you might be delivered from that false idea! Mercy still rules the hour. There is hope while Jesus sends His gospel to you and bids you repent. "I believe in the forgiveness of sins": this is a sweet sentence of a true Christian creed. I believe also in the renewal of men's hearts, for the Lord can give new hearts and right spirits to the evil and unthankful. Do you believe it? Then come to Jesus and receive the blessings of free grace.

We have a number of lepers who come into our church whose disease is white upon their brows and visible to all beholders, and yet *they are indifferent*. They do not mourn their wickedness or wish to be cleansed from it. They sit among God's people, and they listen to the doctrine of a new birth and the news of pardon, and they hear the teaching as though it had nothing to do with them. If now and then they half wish that salvation would come to them, it is too languid a wish to last. They have not yet so perceived their disease and their danger as to pray to be delivered from them. They sleep upon the bed of sloth and care neither for heaven nor for hell. Indifference to spiritual things is the sin of the age. Men are passive of heart about eternal realities. An awful apathy is upon the multitude. The leper in our text was not so foolish as this. He eagerly desired to be delivered from his dreadful malady. With heart and soul the leper yearned to be cleansed from its terrible defilement. Oh, that it were so with you! May the Lord make you feel how depraved your heart is and how diseased with sin are all the faculties of your soul!

Alas, *there are some that even love their leprosy!* Is it not a sad thing to have to say this? Surely, madness is in men's hearts. Men do not wish to be saved from doing evil. They love the ways and wages of iniquity. They would like to go to heaven, but they must have their drunken frolics on the road. They would like to be saved from hell but not from the sin that is the cause of it. Their notion of salvation is not to be saved from the love of evil and to be made pure and clean, but that is God's meaning when He speaks of salvation. How can they hope to be the slaves of sin and yet at the same time be free? Our first necessity is to be saved from sinning. The very name of Jesus tells us *that*: He is called Jesus because "he shall save his people from their sins" (Matt. 1:21). These people do not care for a salvation that would mean self-denial and the giving up of ungodly lusts. O wretched lepers, who count their leprosy to be a beauty and take pleasure in sin, which in the sight of God is far more loathsome than the worst disease of the body! Oh, that Christ Jesus would come and change their view of things until they are of the same mind toward sin as God, who calls it "this abominable thing that I hate" (Jer. 44:4). Oh, if men could see their love for wrong things to be a disease more sickening than leprosy, they would cry out to be saved, and saved at once! Holy Spirit, convince of sin, that sinners may be eager to be cleansed!

Lepers were obliged to stay together: lepers associated with lepers, and they must have made up a dreadful society. How glad they would have been to escape from it! But I know spiritual lepers who *love the company of their fellow lepers.* Yes, and the more leprous a man becomes, the more his fellow lepers admire him. A bold sinner is often the idol of his comrades. Though foul in his life, others cling to him for that very reason. Such persons like to learn some new bit of wickedness, they are eager to be initiated into a yet darker form of impure pleasure. How they long to hear that last lascivious song, to read that last impure novel! It seems to be the desire of many to know as much evil as they can. They flock together, taking dreadful pleasure in talk and action that is the horror of all pure minds. Strange lepers, who heap up leprosy as a treasure! Even those who do not go into gross open sin yet are pleased with unbelieving notions and skeptical opinions, which are a wretched form of mental leprosy. O horrible malady, that makes men doubt the Word of the living God!

Lepers were not allowed to associate with healthy persons except under severe restrictions. Thus they were separated from their nearest and dearest friends. What a sorrow! Alas! I know persons thus separated who *do not wish to associate with the godly.* To them, holy company is dull and wearisome. They do not feel free and easy in such society, and therefore they avoid it as much as decency allows. How can they hope to live with saints forever, when they shun them now as dull and moping acquaintances?

I am writing this in the hope that God would bless the word to someone who feels he is a sinner and desires to be cleansed. Others like the leper, I am seeking with my whole heart. I pray God to bless the word to those who wish to escape from evil company, who would no longer sit in the assembly of the mockers or run in the paths of the unholy. To those who have grown weary of their sinful companions and would escape from them lest they should be bound up in bundles with them to burn at the last great day— to such I write at this time with a loving desire for their salvation. I hope my word will come with divine application to some poor heart that is crying, "I wish I might be numbered with the people of God. I wish I were fit to be a doorkeeper in the house of the Lord. Oh, that my dreadful sinfulness were conquered so that I could have fellowship with the godly and be myself one of them!"

My Lord is looking for such lost ones, that He may find them. I am looking out for them with tearful eyes. But my feeble eyes cannot read inward character, and it is good that the loving Savior, who discerns the secrets of all hearts and reads all inward desires, is looking from the watchtowers of heaven, that He may discover those who are coming to Him, even though as yet they are a great way off. Oh, that sinners may now beg and pray to be rescued from their sins! May those who have become addicted to evil long to break off their evil habits! Happy will the preacher be if he finds himself surrounded with penitents who hate their sins and guilty ones who cry to be forgiven and to be so changed that they shall go and sin no more.

This Leper's Faith Caused Him to Believe That He Could Be Healed of His Hideous Disease

Leprosy was an unutterably loathsome disease. As it exists even now, it is described by those who have seen it in such a way that I will not harrow your feelings by repeating all the sickening details. The following quotation may be more than sufficient. Dr. Thomson in his famous work, "The Land and the Book," speaks of lepers in the East and says, "The hair falls from the head and eyebrows; the nails loosen, decay and drop off; joint after joint of the fingers and toes shrink up and slowly fall away. The gums are absorbed, and the teeth disappear. The nose, the eyes, the tongue and the palate are slowly consumed." The disease turns a man into a mass of loathsomeness. Leprosy is nothing better than a horrible and lingering death. The leper in the narrative before us had sad personal experience of this, and yet he believed that Jesus could cleanse him. Splendid faith! Oh, that you who are afflicted with moral and spiritual leprosy could believe in this fashion! Jesus Christ of Nazareth can heal even you. Over the horror of leprosy, faith triumphed. Oh, that in your case it would overcome the terribleness of sin!

Leprosy was known to be incurable. There was no case of a man's being cured of real leprosy by any medical or surgical treatment. This made the cure of Naaman in former ages so noteworthy. Observe, moreover, that our Savior Himself, so far as I can see, had never healed a leper up to the moment when this poor wretch appeared upon the scene. He had cured fever and cast out devils, but the cure of leprosy was in the Savior's life as yet an unexampled thing. Yet this man, putting this and that together and understanding something of the nature and character of the Lord Jesus Christ, believed that He could cure him of his incurable disease. He felt that even if the great Lord had not yet healed leprosy, He was assuredly capable of doing so great a deed, and he determined to apply to Him. Was not this grand faith? Oh, that such faith could be found at this hour!

Hear me, O trembling sinner: if you are as full of sin as an egg is full of meat, Jesus can remove it all. If your propensities to sin are as untameable as the wild boar of the wood, yet Jesus Christ, the Lord of all, can subdue your iniquities and make you the obedient servant of His love. Jesus can turn the lion into a lamb, and He can do it now. He can transform you where you are sitting, saving you while you read this word. All things are possible to the Savior God, and all things are possible to him who believes. I would you had such a faith as this leper had, although if it were even less, it might be enough, since you have not all his difficulties to contend with, because Jesus has already saved many sinners like yourself and changed many hearts as hard as yours. If He shall regenerate you, He will be doing for you no strange thing but only one of the daily miracles of His grace. He has now healed thousands of your fellow lepers. Can you not believe that He can heal the leprosy in you?

This man had a marvelous faith, thus to believe while *he was personally the victim of that mortal malady*. It is one thing to trust a doctor when you are well, but quite another to confide in him when your body is rotting away. For a real, conscious sinner to trust the Savior is no small thing. When you hope that there is some good thing in you, it is easy to be confident, but to be conscious of total ruin and yet to believe in the divine remedy—this is real faith. To see the sunshine is mere natural vision, but to see in the dark needs the eye of faith. To believe that Jesus has saved you when you see the signs of it, this is the result of reason. But to trust Him to cleanse you while you are still defiled with sin—this is the essence of saving faith.

The leprosy was firmly seated and fully developed in this man. Luke says that he was "full of leprosy" (Luke 5:12). The man had as much of the poison in him as one poor body could contain; it had come to its worst stage in him, and yet he believed that Jesus of Nazareth could make him clean. Glorious confidence! If you are full of sin, if your propensities and habits have become as bad as bad can be, I pray the Holy Spirit to give you faith enough to believe that the Son of God can forgive you and renew you and do it at once. With one word of His mouth, Jesus can turn your death into life, your corruption into beauty. Changes that we cannot work in others, much less in ourselves, Jesus, by His invincible Spirit, can work in the hearts of the ungodly. Of these stones He can raise up children unto Abraham. His moral and spiritual miracles are often wrought upon cases that seem beyond all hope, cases that pity itself endeavors to forget because its efforts have been so long in vain.

I like best about this man's faith that he did not merely believe that Jesus Christ could cleanse a leper but believed that He could cleanse *him!* He said, "Lord, if thou wilt, thou canst make *me* clean." It is very easy to believe for other people. There is really no faith in such impersonal, proxy confidence. The true faith believes for itself first and then for others. Oh, I know some of you are saying, "I believe that Jesus can save my brother. I believe that He can save the vilest of the vile. If I heard that He had saved the biggest drunkard, I should not wonder." Can you believe all this and yet fear that He cannot save you? This is strange inconsistency. If He heals another man's leprosy, can He not heal your leprosy? If one drunkard is saved, why not another? If in one a passionate temper is subdued, why not in another? If lust and covetousness and lying and pride have been cured in many, why not in you? Even if you are a blasphemer, blasphemy has been cured. Why should it not be so in your case? Jesus can heal you of any form of sin that possesses you, however high a degree its power may have reached, for nothing is too hard for the Lord. Jesus can change and cleanse you now. In a moment He can impart a new life and commence a new character. Can you believe this? This is the faith that glorified Jesus and brought healing to this leper, and it is the faith that will save you at once if you now exercise it. O Spirit of the living God, work this faith in the minds of my readers, that they may thus win their suit with the Lord Jesus and go their way healed of the plague of sin.

Faith Is Fixed on Jesus Christ Alone

Let me note the man's words to Jesus again: "If thou wilt, thou canst make me clean." Throw the emphasis upon the pronouns. See the man kneeling before the Lord Jesus and hear him say, "If *thou* wilt, *thou* canst make *me* clean." The man has no intention of looking to the disciples, not to one of them or to all of them. He had had no notion of trusting in a measure to the medicine that physicians would prescribe for him. All that is gone. No dream of other hope remains. But with his eye fully fixed on the blessed Miracle-worker of Nazareth, the leper cries, "If *thou* wilt, *thou* canst make me clean." In himself he had no shade of confidence; every delusion of that kind had been banished by a fierce experience of his disease. He knew that none on earth could deliver him and that by no innate power of constitution could he throw out the poison. But he confidently believed that the Son of God could by himself effect the cure. This was God-given faith—the faith of God's elect—and Jesus was its sole object.

How did this man come to have such faith? I cannot tell you the outward means, but I think we may guess without presumption. *Had he not heard our Lord preach?* Matthew puts this story immediately after the Sermon on the Mount and says, "When he was come down from the mountain, great multitudes followed him. And...there came a leper,...saying, Lord, if thou wilt, thou canst make me clean" (Matt. 8:1–2). Had this man managed to stand at the edge of the crowd and hear Jesus speak, and did those wondrous words convince him that the great Teacher was something more than man? As he noted the style and manner and content of that marvelous sermon, did he say within himself, "Never man spake like this man. Truly He is the Son of God. I believe in Him. I trust Him. He can cleanse me"? May God bless the preaching of Christ crucified to you who hear me! Is not this used of the Lord and made to be the power of God unto salvation to everyone who believes?

Perhaps this man had seen our Lord's miracles. I feel sure he had. He had seen the devils cast out and had heard of Peter's wife's mother, who had lain sick of a fever and been instantaneously recovered. The leper might very properly argue that to heal a fever requires omnipotence; and once granted that omnipotence is at work, then omnipotence can as well deal with leprosy as with fever. Did he not reason well if he argued thus—what the Lord has done, He can do again. If in one case He has displayed almighty power, He can display that same power in another case? Thus would the acts of the Lord corroborate His words and furnish a sure foundation for the leper's hope. Have you not seen Jesus save others? Have you not at least read of His miracles of grace? Believe Him, then, for His works' sake and say to Him, "Lord, if thou wilt, thou canst make me clean."

Besides, I think *this man may have heard something of the story of Christ* and may have been familiar with the Old Testament prophecies concerning the Messiah. It is possible that a disciple may have informed him of John's witness concerning the Christ and of the signs and tokens that supported John's testimony. He may thus have discerned in the Son of Man the Messiah of God, the Incarnate Deity. At any rate, as knowledge must come before faith, the leper had received knowledge enough to feel that he could trust this glorious person and to believe that if He willed it, Jesus could make him clean. O my dear reader, cannot you trust the Lord Jesus Christ in this way? Do you not believe that He is the Son of God, and if so, why not trust Him? He who was born of Mary at Bethlehem was God over all, blessed forever! Do you not believe this? Why, then, do you not rely upon God in our nature? You believe in His consecrated life, His suffering death, His resurrection, His ascension, His sitting in power at the right hand of the Father. Why do you not trust Him? God has highly exalted Him and caused all fullness to dwell in Him. He is able to save to the uttermost, so why do you not come to Him?

Believe that He is able and then, with all your sins before you, like scarlet—and with all your sinful habits and evil propensities before you, ingrained like the leopard's spots—believe that the Savior of men can at once make you whiter than snow as to past guilt and free from the present and future tyranny of evil. A divine Savior must be able to cleanse you from all sin. Only Jesus can do it, but He can do it—do it Himself alone, do it now, do it in you, do it with a word. If Jesus wills to do it, it is all that is needed, for His will is the will of the Almighty Lord. Say, "Lord, if thou wilt, thou canst make me clean." Faith must be fixed alone on Jesus. No other name is given among men whereby we must be saved (Acts 4:12). Jesus is God's ultimatum of salvation: the unique hope of guilty men both as to pardon and as to renewal. Accept Him even now.

This Man's Faith Had Respect to a Real Cure

The leper did not think of the Lord Jesus Christ as a priest who would perform certain ceremonies over him and formally say, "Thou art clean," for that would not have been true. He wanted to have those dry scales, into which his skin kept turning, taken all away, that his flesh might become as the flesh of a little child. He wanted that the rottenness that was eating up his body should be stopped and that health should be actually restored. Friend, it is easy enough to believe in a more priestly absolution if you are gullible enough, but we need more than this. Is it very easy to believe in baptismal regeneration, but what is the good of it? What practical result does it produce? A child remains the same after he has been baptismally regenerated as he was before, and he grows up to prove it. It is easy to believe in sacramentarianism if you are foolish enough, but there is nothing in it when you believe in it. No sanctifying power comes with outward ceremonials in and of themselves. To believe that the Lord Jesus Christ can make us love the good things that once we despised and shun those evil things in which we once took pleasure—this is to believe in Him indeed and of a truth. Jesus can totally change our nature and make a sinner into a saint. This is faith of a practical kind; this is a faith worth having.

None of us would imagine that this leper meant that the Lord Jesus could make him feel comfortable in remaining a leper. Some seem to fancy that Jesus came to let us go on in our sins with a quiet conscience, but He did nothing of the kind. His salvation is cleansing from sin, and if we love sin, we are not saved from it. We cannot have justification without sanctification. There is no use in quibbling about it. There must be a change, a radical change, a change of heart, or else we are not saved. Do you desire a moral and a spiritual change—a change of life, thought, and motive? This is what Jesus gives. Just as this leper needed a thorough physical change, so do you need an entire renewal of your spiritual nature so as to become a new creature in Jesus Christ. The man who desires to be pure is beginning to be pure; the man who sincerely longs to conquer sin has struck the first blow already. The power of sin is shaken in that man who looks to Jesus for deliverance from it. The man who frets under the yoke of sin will not long be a slave to it; if he can believe that Jesus Christ is able to set him free, he shall soon quit his bondage.

Some sins that have hardened down into habits disappear in a moment when Jesus Christ looks upon a man in love. I have known many people who for many years have never spoken without swearing or uttering a filthy expression who, being converted, have never been known to use such language again and have scarcely ever been tempted in that direction. This is one of the sins that seem to die at the first shot, and it is a very wonderful thing it should be so. I have known others who were so changed that the very propensity that was strongest in them has been the last to annoy them afterwards. They have had such a reversal of the mind's action that while other sins have troubled them for years and they have had to set a strict watch against them, their favorite and dominant sin has never again had the slightest influence over them, except to excite an outburst of horror and deep repentance.

Oh, that you had faith in Jesus that He could thus cast down and cast out your reigning sins! Believe in the conquering arm of the Lord Jesus, and He will do it. Conversion is the standing miracle of the Church. Where it is genuine, it is as clear a proof of divine power going with the gospel as was the casting out of devils or even the raising of the dead in our Lord's day. We see these conversions still and have proof that Jesus is still able to work great moral marvels. So where are you? Can you not believe that Jesus is able to make a new person of you? Receive the grace to believe in the Lord Jesus for purification of heart, pardon of sin, and the implantation of eternal life. Then when faith is given, the Lord Jesus will work your sanctification, and none shall effectually hinder.

This Man's Faith Had a Measure of Hesitancy

He said, "If thou wilt, thou canst make me clean." There was an "if" in this speech, and that "if" has aroused the suspicions of many preachers. Some think it supposes that he doubted our Lord's willingness. I hardly think that the language justly bears so harsh a construction. What he meant may have been this—"Lord, I do not know yet if You are sent to heal lepers. I have not seen that You have ever done so. But, still, if it is within the compass of Your commission, I believe You will do it, and assuredly You can if You will. You can heal not only some lepers, but me in particular. You can make me clean." I think this was a legitimate thing for him to say, as he had not seen a leper healed.

Moreover, I admire in this text *the deference that the leper pays to the sovereignty of Christ's will as to the bestowal of His gifts.* To say, "If thou wilt, thou canst make me clean," was as much as to say, "I know You have a right to distribute these great favors exactly as You please. I have no claim upon You. I cannot say that You are bound to make me clean. I appeal to Your pity and free favor. The matter remains with Your will." The man had never read the verse, "It is not of him that willeth, nor of him that runneth, but of God that sheweth mercy" (Rom. 9:16), for it was not yet written, but he had in his mind the humble spirit suggested by that grand truth. He owned that grace must come as a free gift of God's good pleasure when he said, "Lord, if thou wilt."

Beloved, we need never raise a question as to the Lord's will to give grace when we have the will to receive it. But still, I would have every sinner feel that he has no claim upon God for anything. If the Lord should give us up, as He did the heathen described in Romans one, we deserve it. If He should never look upon us with an eye of love, what could we say against His righteous sentence? We have willfully sinned and deserve to be left in our sin. Confessing all this, we still cling to our firm belief in the power of grace and cry, "Lord, if thou wilt, thou canst." We appeal to our Savior's pitying love, relying upon His boundless power.

See, also, how the leper *really speaks without hesitancy* if you understand him. He does not say, "Lord, if thou puttest out thy hand, thou canst make me clean," or, "Lord, if thou speakest, thou canst make me clean," but only, "Lord, *if thou wilt*, thou canst make me clean." Christ's mere will can do it. Oh, splendid faith! If you are inclined to doubting, I would have you admire the leper for running so well with a lame foot. If there was a weakness anywhere in his faith, still his faith was so strong that the weakness only manifests its strength. Sinner, it is so, and I pray God that your heart may grasp it—if the Lord wills it, He can make you clean. Do you believe this? If so, carry out practically what your faith will suggest to you—namely, that you come to Jesus and plead with Him and get from Him the cleansing that you need. To that end I am hoping to lead you as the Holy Spirit shall enable me.

This Man's Faith
Had Earnest Action Flowing Out of It

Believing that if Jesus willed He could make him clean, what did the leper do? At once he came to Jesus. I know not from what distance, but he came as near to Jesus as he could. Then we read that he sought Jesus; that is to say, he pleaded, and pleaded, and pleaded again. He cried, "Lord, cleanse me! Lord, heal my leprosy!" Nor was this all. He fell on his knees and worshiped, for we read, "Kneeling down to him." He not only knelt, but he knelt to

Jesus. He had no difficulty as to paying Him divine honor. He worshiped the Lord Christ, paying Him reverent homage. He then went on to honor Him by an open acknowledgement of His marvelous power, His infinite power, by saying, "Lord, if thou wilt, thou canst make me clean." I should not wonder whether some who stood by began to smile at what they thought to be the poor man's fanatical credulity. These skeptics murmured, "What a poor fool this leper is, to think that Jesus of Nazareth can cure him of his leprosy!" Such a confession of faith had seldom been heard. But whatever critics and skeptics might think, this brave man boldly declared, "Lord, this is my confession of faith. I believe that if thou wilt, thou canst make me clean."

If you are full of guilt and hardened in sin and yet anxious to be healed, look straightway to the Lord Jesus Christ. He is here now. In the preaching of the gospel, He is with us always. With the eyes of your mind, behold Him, for He beholds you. You know that He lives, even though you see Him not. Believe in this living Jesus; believe for perfect cleansing. Cry to Him, worship Him, adore Him, trust Him. He is very God of very God. Bow before Him and cast yourself upon His mercy. Go to your knees and say, "Lord, I believe that You can make me clean." He will hear your cry and will save you. There will be no interval between your prayer and the gracious reward of faith.

His Faith Had Its Reward

Have patience with me just a minute. The reward of this man's faith was first, that *his very words were treasured up*. Matthew, Mark, and Luke—all three of them—record the precise words that this man used: "Lord, if thou wilt, thou canst make me clean." They evidently did not see so much to find fault within them as some have done. On the contrary, they thought them gems to be placed in the setting of their gospels. Three times over are they recorded because they are such a splendid confession of faith for a poor, diseased leper to have made. I believe that God is as much glorified by that one sentence of the leper as by the song of cherubim and seraphim, when they continually cry, "Holy, holy, holy, is the Lord of hosts" (Isa. 6:3). A sinner's lips declaring his confident faith in God's own

Son can breathe sonnets unto God more sweet than those of the angelic choirs. This man's first faith words are folded up in the fair linen of three gospel writers and laid up in the treasury of the house of the Lord. God values the language of humble confidence.

His next reward was that *Jesus echoed his words.* He said, "Lord, if thou wilt, thou canst make me clean"; and Jesus said, "I will; be thou clean." As an echo answers to the voice, so did Jesus to His supplicant. The Lord Jesus was so pleased with this man's words that He caught them as they leaped out of his mouth and used them Himself, saying, "I will; be thou clean." If you can get, then, only as far as this leper's confession, I believe that our Lord Jesus from His throne above will answer your prayer.

So potent were the words of this leper that *they moved our Lord very wonderfully.* Read the forty-first verse: "And Jesus, moved with compassion." The Greek word expresses a stirring of the entire manhood, a commotion in all the inward parts. The heart and all the vitals of the man are in active movement. The Savior was greatly moved. You have seen a man moved, have you not? When a strong man is unable any longer to restrain himself and is forced to give way to his feelings, you have seen him tremble all over and at last burst out into an evident breakdown. It was just so with the Savior—His pity moved Him, His delight in the leper's faith mastered Him. When He heard the man speak with such confidence in Him, the Savior was moved with a sacred passion that, as it was in sympathy with the leper, is called "compassion." Oh, to think that a poor leper should have such power over the divine Son of God! Yet, in all your sin and misery, if you can believe in Jesus, you can move the heart of your blessed Savior. Yes, even now His heart yearns toward you.

No sooner was our Lord Jesus thus moved than *out went His hand,* and He touched the man and healed him immediately. It did not require a long time for the working of the cure, but the leper's blood was cleansed in a single second. Our Lord could work this miracle and make all things new in the man, for "all things were made by him; and without him was not any thing made that was made" (John 1:3). Jesus restored the poor, decaying, putrefying body of this man, and the man was cleansed at once.

To make the man quite sure that he was cleansed, the Lord

Jesus bade him go to the priest and seek a certificate of health. The man was so clean that he could be examined by the appointed sanitary authority and come off without suspicion. The cure that he had received was a real and radical one, and therefore he might go away at once and get the certificate of it. If our converts will not bear practical tests, they are worth nothing. Let even our enemies judge whether they are not better men and women when Jesus has renewed them. If Jesus saves a sinner, He does not mind all men testing the change. Jesus does not seek display, but He seeks examination from those able to judge. Our converts will bear the test. Come hither, angels! Come hither, pure intelligences, able to observe men in secret! Here is a wretch of a sinner who seemed first cousin to the devil, but the Lord Jesus Christ has converted him and changed him. Now look at him, you angels; look at him at home in his chamber! Watch him in private life. We can read your verdict. "There is joy in the presence of the angels of God over one sinner that repenteth" (Luke 15:10), and this proves what you think. It is such a wonderful change, and angels are so sure of it, that they give their certificates at once. How do they give their certificates? Why, each one manifests his joy as he sees the sinner turning from his sinful ways. Oh, that the angels might have work of this kind at this moment!

Dear reader, may you be one over whom the angels rejoice! If you believe on Jesus Christ, and if you will trust Him as the sent One of God, fully and entirely with your soul, He will make you clean. Behold Him on the cross, and see sin put away. Behold Him risen from the dead, and see new life bestowed. Behold Him enthroned in power, and see evil conquered. Believe your Savior, and your cure is wrought. God help you, for Jesus Christ's sake!

The Lord had told His disciples to make for the other side, and therefore they did their best and continued rowing all night, making no progress whatsoever because the wind was dead against them. It was with difficulty that they maintained the little distance they had made and were not blown back again to the starting place. You may have heard it said that if a Christian does not go forward, he goes backward. That statement is not altogether true, for there are times of a spiritual trial when, if a man does not go backward, he is really going forward. "Stand fast" is a precept that, when well kept, may involve as much virtue as "press forward." A ship's captain will give full throttle and drive right into the teeth of a hurricane and remain perfectly satisfied if the good ship can only keep from being driven on shore. The apostolic crew rowed and rowed and rowed, and it was no fault of theirs that they made no progress, "for the wind was contrary unto them." The Christian man may make little or no headway, and yet it may be no fault of his, for the wind is contrary. Our good Lord will take the will for the deed and reckon our progress—not by our apparent advance but by the hearty intent with which we tug at the oars.

· Chapter Nine

Good Cheer from
Christ's Real Presence

*And straightway he constrained his disciples to get into the ship,
and to go to the other side before unto Bethsaida, while he sent
away the people. And when he had sent them away, he departed
into a mountain to pray. And when even was come, the ship was
in the midst of the sea, and he alone on the land. And he saw
them toiling in rowing; for the wind was contrary unto them:
and about the fourth watch of the night he cometh unto them,
walking upon the sea, and would have passed by them. But when
they saw him walking upon the sea, they supposed it had been a
spirit, and cried out: For they all saw him, and were troubled.
And immediately he talked with them, and saith unto them, Be of
good cheer: it is I; be not afraid. And he went up unto them into
the ship; and the wind ceased: and they were sore amazed in
themselves beyond measure, and wondered. For they considered
not the miracle of the loaves: for their heart was hardened.*

—Mark 6:45–52.

WE HAVE HERE A WORD of comfort given to
a shipload of believers *who were where their Lord had sent them.* They
had been unwilling to put out to sea, though it was probably calm
enough at the time, but they did not wish to leave the Lord Jesus.

He constrained them to go, and thus their sailing was not merely under His sanction but was by His express command. They were in their right place, and yet they met with a terrible storm. The little inland sea upon which they sailed lies in a deep hollow, and from the shore there pours a sudden downdraft of tremendous wind for which it is not possible to be prepared. By one of these whirlwinds the whole sea was stirred up to boiling, as only those little lakes can be. So, though they were where Jesus commanded them to go, they were in desperate peril, and you, dear friend, must not think that you are in a wrong position because you are in trouble. Do not consider that adverse circumstances are a proof that you have missed your road. Adversity may even be an evidence that you are in the good old way, since the path of believers is seldom without trial. You did well to embark and to leave the shore; but remember, though your Lord has insured the vessel and guaranteed that you shall reach your haven, He has not promised that you shall sail over a sea of glass. On the contrary, He has told you that "in the world ye shall have tribulation" (John 16:33), and you may all the more confidently believe in Him because you find His warning to be true.

The Lord had told His disciples to make for the other side, and therefore they did their best and continued rowing all night, making no progress whatsoever because the wind was dead against them. It was with difficulty that they maintained the little distance they had made and were not blown back again to the starting place. You may have heard it said that if a Christian does not go forward, he goes backward. That statement is not altogether true, for there are times of a spiritual trial when, if a man does not go backward, he is really going forward. "Stand fast" is a precept that, when well kept, may involve as much virtue as "press forward." A ship's captain will give full throttle and drive right into the teeth of a hurricane and remain perfectly satisfied if the good ship can only keep from being driven on shore. The apostolic crew rowed and rowed and rowed, and it was no fault of theirs that they made no progress, "for the wind was contrary unto them." The Christian man may make little or no headway, and yet it may be no fault of his, for the wind is contrary. Our good Lord will take the will for the deed and reckon our progress—not by our apparent advance but by the hearty intent with which we tug at the oars.

Often, when a believer groans in prayer and cannot pray, he has offered the best prayer. When he tries to win men's hearts and does not win them, his zeal is as acceptable as if it convinced a nation. And when he would wish to do good but finds evil present with him, there is good in the desire. If he threw up the oars and drifted with the wind, that would be another thing. But if our Lord sees him "toiling in rowing," although no progress is made, He has never a word to say against His servant, but He will say to him, "Be of good cheer."

It does not appear from the biblical narrative that the disciples had any fear about the storm, except such as might naturally arise even in the minds of fishermen when they were dreadfully tossed upon the sea. The disciples probably said to one another, "Did not our Master constrain us to set forth on this voyage? Though we meet with this storm, we are not to be blamed." Certain believers who have recently come to faith in Christ have been great losers in worldly things by becoming Christians. What then? Let them not be terrified by this fact; even Christ's ship is tossed with tempest. Let them row on against the wind. If the storm increases in fury, let them not lose heart. One who knew the seas very well exclaimed, "Though he slay me, yet will I trust in him" (Job 13:15). In so doing, he glorified God and before long found himself in a great calm. Does Jesus bid us make for the shore? Then let us row on, even if we cannot make headway, for Jesus knows all about it and orders all things well.

Why, then, did our Savior, when He came to this shipboard of apostles who had been toiling and rowing, say to them, "Be of good cheer"? They were bold, brave men and were not at all afraid of the sea. What, then, did they fear? He would not have spoken like this unless they had been afraid of something. On looking at the text, we see to our astonishment that *they were afraid of Jesus Himself.* They were not afraid of winds and storms and waves and tempests, but they were afraid of their best friend. That is the point at which He aimed by saying, "Be of good cheer: *it is I;* be not afraid."

We will first consider *the cause of their fear*. Then we will meditate upon *the method by which Jesus cheered them*. And, finally, we will reflect upon *the times when we shall need just such a good word as this*.

The Cause of Their Fear

If we had not sailed over the same lake, it might have surprised us that they were afraid of their Lord. Jesus was appearing for them and coming to their rescue. He was about to still the tempest for them, yet they were afraid of Him—of Him whom they loved and trusted. Their hearts were so hardened that they were afraid of their Lord, and afraid of Him when He was giving them the best reason for trusting Him. Before their eyes He was displaying Himself as Lord over all, Master of wind and wave, and yet they were afraid of Him. The greatness of His power would have comforted them had they understood the truth. But they did not consider the miracle of the loaves, and therefore they were in a state of perplexity and were extremely afraid.

Meanwhile, Jesus was acting in great gentleness toward them. He was displaying His power, but it was not in a dazzling and overwhelming manner. Admire the sacred gentleness that made Him move as though He would have passed by them. If He had suddenly appeared in brilliant light in the middle of the ship, He might have astounded them and driven them to fright. If He had suddenly shone forth just at the stern or alighted from the heavens upon the deck, they would have been petrified with alarm. But He begins by showing Himself way out there on the crest of the billow, and one cries to his fellow, "See that strange light yonder?" They watch, and Jesus comes nearer! They can discern a figure. They can see a man step from wave to wave with a majestic tread.

In tenderness, Jesus will not flash upon them all at once. As when the morning breaks by a slow increase of light, so Jesus comes to His timid followers. Even then, He moves as though He would pass by them, that they might not be alarmed by His appearing to bear down upon them as an adversary. Even so, He manifests himself to us in the riches of His grace in all wisdom and prudence.

The fears of the trembling crew were sufficiently aroused by even seeing Him at a distance. They were so afraid that they cried out thinking that they saw a ghost. What would they have done had He not, in gentleness to their weakness, manifested Himself gradually to them and set Himself in a sidelight? Take what way the Master might, His disciples were still afraid, and we are not much wiser or much more courageous than they were. The manifestation of the Christ of God to us in all His glory will have to be by degrees as long as we are in this body. And perhaps, even in heaven, it may not be at the very first that we shall be able to endure the fullness of its joy. Even there, He may have to lead us to the fountains of water that at the first we did not discover, and guide us into more and more of that superlative knowledge that will utterly eclipse all acquaintance that we have of Him now, as the sunlight puts out the stars.

How much are we like the disciples? They were afraid of Jesus when He was revealing His power to help them. Afraid of Him when He was acting in the gentlest possible manner toward them and treating them as a nurse does her child. Ah me, that we should be afraid of Jesus!

The Lord, after all, was doing nothing more than they knew He could do. Twenty-four hours had not passed since they had seen Him perform a work of creation, for He had taken bread and fish, then multiplied them so as to make a festival for five thousand men, besides women and children. After this miracle, they should not have been surprised that He should traverse the sea. To walk the waters is to suspend a law, but to make loaves and fishes is to exercise the supreme power of creation, which must forever remain with God Himself. Knowing this, they should not have been astonished—not so soon, at any rate. The memory of that festival should not have vanished quite so quickly from the most forgetful minds. Yet when they saw Him only doing what they knew He could do, only doing something not a jot more difficult than He was accustomed to do, they cried out for fear.

Was it not because *they dreaded contact with the spiritual, the mysterious, and the supernatural?* Although we are talking now about them, and perhaps half saying in our minds, "If we had been there, we would not have been afraid of Jesus and cried out," we do not know what we say. It takes very little of the supernatural to make a man's flesh creep, no matter who the man is. When Belshazzar saw the hand writing upon the wall (Dan. 5:5), he trembled most because of the mystery involved in a moving hand with which no visible body was connected. The unseen is the birthplace of fear. Imagination exaggerates, and conscience whispers that some great evil will befall us. We are nearing the confines of the mysterious world where God and spirits dwell, and therefore we tremble. Yet, the spirit world is the last thing that Christians should tremble at, for there can be nothing in the supernatural world that we have cause to dread. If there is such a thing as a ghost walking the earth, I, for one, should like to meet it—either at the dead of night or the noon of day.

I have not the least particle of faith in rambling spirits. Those who are in heaven will not care to be wandering in these foggy regions, and those in hell cannot leave their dread abode. From where, then, shall they come? Are they devils? Even so, and what then? A devil is no new personage. We have fought with devils often enough and are prepared to resist them again and make them fly. The Lord will tread Satan, who is the master of evil spirits, under our feet shortly (Rom. 16:20); why, then, should we be afraid of his underlings? Nothing supernatural should cause any Christian the slightest alarm. We are expressly forbidden to fear the fear of the heathen, and one of their greatest horrors is the dread of witchcraft and necromancy and other supposed manifestations of evil spirits. We who believe in Jesus are to be ashamed of such a fear, lest a lie should have dominion over us.

If saintly spirits and holy angels can appear among men, what then? It would be a joy and a privilege to meet them. We are come to an innumerable company of angels (Heb. 12:22) who bear us up in their hands lest we dash our feet against a stone (Luke 4:11).

Personally, I am more afraid of the natural than of the supernatural, and far more fearful of the carnal than of the spiritual. Yet the disciples were afraid of Jesus because they were fearful of the supernatural. When a person falls under that dread, he will be afraid of anything. I have known people to be frightened by cattle, alarmed by a cat, and distressed at the croak of a raven. Some foolish ones have even died with fear at the click of an insect in an old post, for they call it a "death watch." Let us put off all such child-ish folly, for if we once fall into it, we may even go the length of these apostles and be afraid of our Master Himself.

How Our Master Cheered His Followers When They Were Afraid

First of all, *He assured them that He was not a disembodied spirit.* He said, "It is I," and that "I" was a man who ate and drank with them, a man of flesh and blood whom they had seen and heard and touched. They were comforted when they knew that it was really no disembodied spirit, but a man in flesh and blood.

I beg you always to remember that Jesus Christ is not to be regarded as an unclothed spirit, for He wears a body like our own. It would greatly detract from our comfort if we doubted the real personality of Christ and the truth of His resurrection. Our Lord has taken into heaven our human nature in its entirety—body as well as soul. He ever lives, not as a spirit but as a man like our-selves, all sin excepted. And He lives in heaven as the pledge that we shall be there too in the completeness of our manhood when the trumpet of the resurrection sounds.

As a real man, Jesus reigns above. He is no phantom, no ghost, no spirit, but a risen man, touched with the feeling of our infirmi-ties, who pities and loves and feels for us. In that capacity, He speaks to us out of the glory of heaven and says, "It is I; be not afraid."

Another thought lies on the surface of the passage; *Jesus com-forted them by the assurance that it was really Himself.* They were not looking upon a delusion; they were looking upon Christ Himself. Friend, be sure of the reality of the Christ you trust in. It is very easy to use the name of Jesus, but not quite so easy to know His person. It is common to talk about what He did, but not to feel that He lives just as truly as we do and that He is a person to be loved and trusted, just as much as our own brother or father or friend. We want a real, living, personal Christ! A phantom Christ will not cheer us in a storm but is rather the cause of fright than hope. But a real Christ is a real consolation in a real tempest. May you truly know the personal Savior to whom you can speak with as much certainty as if you could touch His hand!

The Christ of 2,000 years ago accomplished our salvation, but the Christ of today must apply it, or we are lost. Seeing that He ever lives, He is able to save to the uttermost them that come unto God by Him (Heb. 7:25). Believe in His true manhood and never allow your idea of Him to become thin and unsubstantial. Those are substantial Christians to whom Christ is substantial.

The source of the comfort lay in this: He said, "It is I; be not afraid," which being interpreted means, *it is Jesus,* be not afraid. When our Lord met Paul on the road to Damascus, He said to Paul, "I am Jesus" (Acts 9:5). But when He spoke to those who knew His voice and were familiar with Him, He did not quote His name but said, "It is I." They were sheep who had been long enough with the Shepherd to know His voice. They had only to hear Him speak, and without a name being mentioned, they perceived that it was the Lord. To this conclusion they should have come at first. But as they blundered and said, "It is a spirit," the loving Master corrected them by saying, "It is I—it is Jesus." It is not possible for me to convey to you what richness of consolation lies at the thought that Jesus is Jesus, which is, being interpreted, the Savior. That one character and office is cheering, but the same is true of all the names He wears. All the glorious titles and the blessed emblems under which He is set forth are rich in good cheer. It is Jesus who walks the water of your trouble and comes to you—Jesus the Son of God, the Alpha and the Omega, the Head over all things to His Church, the All-in-all of all His people.

When Jesus wished to encourage John in the first chapter of the Revelation, the comfort He gave was, "I am the first and the last" (vs. 17). The comfort of the Lord's people lies in the person and character of Jesus. Here is their solace: "It is I." But what a big "I" it is. Compound in one all that is conceivable of goodness and mercy and grace and faithfulness and love. Add perfect humanity and infinite Godhead and all the sovereign rights, powers, and possessions of the Highest, and these are all contained in the one little letter "I" when Jesus says, "It is I; be not afraid."

But you have not reached the bottom of it yet. The literal rendering of the Greek is "*I am.*" The word that Jesus said was not "It is I," but "I am." When He would cheer His ancient people, the

Lord told Moses to comfort Israel by saying, "I AM hath sent me unto you" (Exod. 3:14). The self-existence of their God was to be the joy of the tribes. When Jesus said to those who came to take Him in the garden, "I am," they fell backward, such was the power of that word (John 18:6). But when He said to these, His cowering disciples, "I am," they were drawn toward Him, and yet they did not lose the awe that must ever go with that incommunicable name "I AM."

Believer, Jesus speaks to you: "I am." Have you lost a loved one? Have your possessions failed? Is your health departing? Are your joys declining? Alas! It is a dying, fleeting world, but there is One who is always the same, for Jesus says to you, "I am; and because I live, you shall live also" (John 14:19). Be comforted; whatever else is gone, wherever else the arrows of death may fly, your Jesus still lives. "I am" is a blessed word of rich comfort to be heard amid the darkness of the night by weary mariners whose spirits had been sinking within them.

The glory of it all was brought out by the fact that "Jesus went up unto them in the ship," and as he stood in their midst, the stillness all around proved that the I AM was there. Had He not moved upon the face of the deep, as once the Spirit moved there, and did there not come order out of the tempest's chaos even as at the beginning? Where the great I AM is present, the winds and the waves perceive their Ruler and obey Him.

Then the disciples knew that Jesus was not only I AM, but also "Immanuel, God with us." I AM had come to their rescue and was in the ship with them. Here, dear friend, is *your* comfort and mine. We will not fear the supernatural or the unseen, for we see Jesus, and in Him we see the Father, and therefore we are of good cheer.

There Are Times When We Shall Need This Same Comfort

Jesus spoke this message to believers who were tossed with a tempest, and we need it *when we are depressed by the surroundings of these evil times.* In seasons of depressed trade, great sickness, terrible wars, and public disasters, it is balm to the spirit to know that Jesus is still the same. Sin may abound yet more, the light of the gospel may burn low, and the prince of darkness may widely sway his destroying scepter, but, nevertheless, this truth stands sure, that Jesus is the I AM. At certain periods, diabolical influence seems paramount. The reins of nations appear to be taken out of the hand of the great Governor, and yet it is not so. Look through the darkness, and you shall see your Lord amid the hurricane, walking the waters of politics, ruling national convulsions, governing, overruling, arranging all, making even the wrath of man to praise Him, and restraining it according to His wisdom. Above the howling of the blast I hear His voice announcing, "It is I." When men's hearts sink for fear and the rowers feel their oars ready to snap by the strain of useless toil, I hear the word that is the soul of music: "It is I; be not afraid. I am ruling all things. I am coming to the rescue of the ship, my Church; she shall yet float on smooth waters and reach her desired haven."

Another time of need will surely be *when we reach the swellings of the Jordan.* As we shall get near the spirit world and the soul will begin to strip off her physical garment to enter on a new form of life, how shall we feel as we enter the unknown world? Shall we cry out, "It is a Spirit!" as we see the first who meets us? It may be so, but then a sweet voice will destroy death's terror and end all our alarms, and this shall be its utterance: "It is I; be not afraid." This new world is not new to Jesus; our pains and dying throes are not unknown to Him! The disembodied state, wherein the spirit sojourns for a while unclothed, He knows it all, for He died and entered into the spirit land and can sympathize with us in every step of the way. In what sweet company shall we pass through the valley of death! Surely its gloom will turn to brightness, as when a cavern, wrapped in blackness, is lit up with a hundred torches and myriads of gems sparkle from roof and walls. Passing through the sepulchre, its damp darkness shall flash and glow with unexpected joys and marvelous revelations of the Ever-blessed, because Jesus will be with us, and "the Lamb is the light" (Rev. 21:23.) If, in that dread hour, we shall feel the least trembling at our Lord as the Judge of all the earth, that dread shall vanish as He cries, "It is I."

This comfort may serve us *when we suffer great tribulation.* May you, my friend, be spared this trial if God so wills. But should it come, you will all the better understand me. Those who "do business in great waters" (Ps. 107:23) know that our troubles are, at times, so pressing that we lose our heads and are not able to cope with our trials. Forebodings fill the air, and our sinking spirits chill the very marrow of our life. We become like distraught men, or as David put it, we reel to and fro, and stagger like a drunken man, and are at our wits' end (Ps. 107:27). Then, ah then, the voices of our comrades in the ship are of little value, and even the echoes of former words from the Lord are of small account. Nothing will serve but the present and sure consolations of the Lord Jesus. We must hear him say, "It is I," or we shall faint outright. Then is the soul braced to withstand the next billow, and while she cries, "All thy waves and thy billows are gone over me" (Ps. 42:7), she is still able to add, "Yet the LORD will command his lovingkindness in the daytime, and in the night his song shall be with me" (Ps. 42:8). When Jesus is with a man, troubles have lost their power to trouble him.

We shall need this same word of comfort *whenever the Lord graciously reveals Himself to us.* His glory is such that we are not able to bear much of it. Its very sweetness overpowers the heart. Saints have had to ask for a staying of the intense delight that seemed to overpower their natural faculties. Those who have enjoyed those transporting manifestations can quite understand why John has written, "When I saw him, I fell at his feet as dead" (Rev. 1:17). An awful delight—or shall I say a delightful awe?—throws the man upon his face. John had lain in Jesus' bosom, and yet, when he had a clear manifestation of his glorified Savior, he could not bear it till his tender Friend laid His hand upon him and said, "Fear not." So it will be with each of us when we are favored with the visits of the Well-beloved; we shall greatly need that He should say to us, "It is I, your Brother, your Friend, your Savior, your Husband; be not afraid. Great as I am, tremble not in My presence, for I am Jesus, the Lover of your soul."

Once more, there is a day coming *when the Son of man will be revealed in the clouds of heaven.* We know not when it will be, but we are solemnly warned that when men are not looking for Him, He will suddenly appear. He will come as a thief in the night to the mass of men. But as for believers, they are not in darkness that that day should come upon them as a thief. To them He comes as a long-expected friend. When He comes, there will be signs in the heavens above and in the earth beneath, which we shall recognize. We may then, perhaps, be distressed by these supernatural portents and begin to tremble. What, then, will be our delight when we hear Him say, "It is I; be not afraid!"

Lift up your head, for the coming of the Lord draws near, and to you it is not darkness, but day. To you it is not judgment and condemnation, but honor and reward. What bliss it will be to catch the first glimpse of our Lord on the throne! Sinners will wring their hands and weep and wail because of Him. But we shall know His voice and welcome His appearing. When the last trumpet rings out clear and loud, happy shall we be to hear that gladsome sound: "It is I; be not afraid." Rolling earth and crumbling mountains, darkened sun and blackened moon, flames of fire and shocks of earthquake, gathering angels and chariots of God, none of these things shall amaze us while Jesus whispers to our soul, "I am," and yet again, "IT IS I; BE NOT AFRAID."

I should think that it was a great marvel to them that a calm was sent so soon after the storm. Man needs time, but God's Word runs very quickly. Man travels with weary steps, but the Lord rides upon a cherub and flies upon the wings of the wind. The particles of air and the drops of water were all in confusion through the tempest, rushing as if chaos had come again, rising in whirlwinds and falling in cataracts, yet they did but see the face of their Maker, and they were still. In one single instant there was a calm. Have not you and I experienced instantaneous workings of divine grace upon our spirits? It may not be so with all, but some of us at the first instant of our faith lost the burden of sin in a moment. Our load was all gone before we knew where we were. The change from sorrow to joy was not worked in us by degrees, but in a moment, the sun leaped above the horizon and the night of our soul was over. Has it not been so since? We have been in the midst of God's people with a heavy spirit and without power to enjoy a truth or to perform a holy act. The hymns seemed a mockery and the prayer an empty form, and yet in a single moment, the rod of the Lord has touched the rock and the waters have flowed forth, and by the very means of grace that seemed so dull and powerless, we have been enlivened and comforted.

Chapter Ten

With the Disciples
on the Lake of Galilee

But the men marvelled, saying, What manner of man is this, that even the winds and the sea obey him! —Matthew 8:27.

And they feared exceedingly, and said one to another, What manner of man is this, that even the wind and the sea obey him? —Mark 4:41.

THIS STORY OF THE tempest upon the lake is wonderfully full of spiritual interest. Not only does it literally show us the divine power of our blessed Master in stilling the tempest, rendered the more conspicuous by being placed side by side with the human weakness that made Him sleep in the ship upon a pillow, but spiritually, it is a kind of ecclesiastical history, a miniature outline of the story of the Church in all ages. Nay, the teaching does not end when you have read the incident in that light. It also contains a suggestive forecast of the story of every man who is making the spiritual voyage in company with Jesus.

Notice, first, how it is a kind of ecclesiastical history. There is Christ in the vessel with His disciples. What is that but a church with its pastor? We see in the church a vessel bearing a rich cargo, steering for a desired haven, and equipped for fishing on the way should fair opportunity occur. Her being upon a sea shows her to be here below, subject to trial, suffering, labor, and peril. I hardly know of any appropriate picture of a church than a ship upon the treacherous Galilean sea with Jesus and His disciples sailing in it. After a while comes a tempest: this we may safely reckon upon.

Whatever ship makes a fair voyage with a favoring wind, the ship of the church never will. She has her calms, but these do not last forever. Her sail is sure to be weather-beaten at one time or another, and the occasions are seldom far apart. The vessel that has Jesus for its captain is destined to feel the tempest. Christ has not come to send peace on earth, but a sword (Matt. 10:34): that is His own declaration, and He knows His own intent. Every sail of the good ship that bears the flag of the Lord High Admiral of our fleet must be beaten with the wind, and every plank in her must be tried by the waves.

To Christ's Church there are many storms, and some of them are the most terrible character. Of heresy: ah, how near to wrecking has she been with the false doctrines of Gnosticism, Arianism, Popery, and Rationalism! Of persecution she has constant experience, but sometimes exceeding intense has the tornado been. In the early stages of Church history, the pagan persecutions of Rome followed thick and fast upon each other. And when Giant Pagan had emptied out all his fury, there came a worse tyrant, whose magical arts raised hurricanes of wind against the good ship. There sat at Rome a harlot who persecuted the saints exceedingly, being drunken with their blood. Then there raged a cyclone that almost drove the boat out of the water and drenched and nearly drowned her crew. Tears and blood covered the saints as with a salt and crimson spray. Hers was no pleasure trip, but she went forth like the lifeboat, fashioned for the purpose of outriding the tempest. The true ship of the Lord was, and is, and will be in a storm until the Lord shall come; and then there shall be for it no further wave of trial, but the sea of glass forever.

Note, again, that while this tempest was roaring worse and worse, the Lord was in the ship, but He seemed to be asleep. So has it often been. No providence delivered the persecuted. No marvelous manifestations of the Spirit scattered the heresy. The Christ was in the Church, but He was in the lower part with His head upon a pillow, asleep. You all know the portions of Church history that this illustrates.

Then came distress: the people in the vessel began to be alarmed and were afraid that they should utterly perish. And do you wonder at it when the peril was so great? That distress led to prayer. Mighty prayer has often been produced by mighty trial. Oh, how slack has the Church been in the presentation of her spiritual offering until the Lord has sent fire upon her, and that fire has seemed to kindle her frankincense so that it has begun to smoke toward heaven! Prayer was produced by distress, and prayer brought distress to an end.

Then arose the Master and displayed His power and Godhead. You know how He has done so in reformations and revivals time after time. He has rebuked the unbelief of His trembling saints, and then He has hushed the winds and the waves, and there has been a time of calm and peace for His poor, weather-beaten Church, a period free from bloodshed and heresy, an area of progress and peace. The Church has a history that has many a time repeated itself. If you take an interest in the navigation of that wondrous vessel that carries Christ and all His chosen, you will never have to complain of a lack of incidents.

But I also said that the story of the storm upon the lake is an admirable emblem of the spiritual voyage of every man who is bound for the fair havens in company with Jesus. We are with Christ, happy with Him, and sailing pleasantly: will this last? Soon comes a storm; the ship rocks and reels; she is covered with waves. It looks as if our frail ship would sink to the bottom. Yet Jesus is in our hearts, and that is our safety. We are saved not by seamanship but by having on board the Lord paramount, who rules all winds and waves and never yet lost a vessel that bore the cross at its masthead.

Sometimes within our hearts He seems to be asleep. We hear not His voice. We see but little of His face. His eyes are closed, and He Himself is hidden away out of sight. He has not altogether left us, blessed be His Name, but He appears to be asleep. Then the ship rocks again, and we reel again, and we wonder that He still can sleep. Then are we driven in great alarm to prayer, to which we should have availed ourselves long before. It may be that we have been busy with ropes and tackle, strengthening the mast, furling the sail, doing all kinds of necessary work, and therefore leaving undone the most necessary work of all, namely, seeking out the Master and telling Him the story of our peril. We pray not till we are forced to our knees, sad sinners that we are. The boat will go down! She will go down!

Now it is that we also go down to the cabin and begin to wake Him up with, "Master, save us: we perish!" Then you know what happens, how the gentle rebuke passes over our spirit, and we are humbled. But the grander rebuke is heard by winds and waves, and they are quieted and sleep at the Master's feet, and in us and around us there is a great calm. How profound the peace! How blessed the stillness! We are about to say, "Would God it would last forever"; but as yet tranquility cannot be perpetual. Our perils of waters will be sure to repeat themselves. Often we go down to the sea in ships and do business in great waters, so that we see the works of the Lord and His wonders in the deep. Hear how a poet sings the story:

> Fierce was the wild billow;
> Dark was the night;
> Oars labour'd heavily;
> Foam glimmer'd white;
> Trembled the mariners;
> Peril was nigh;
> Then said the God of God,
> "Peace! It is I!"

> Ridge of the mountain-wave,
> Lower thy crest!
> Wail of Euroclydon,
> Be thou at rest!
> Sorrow can never be,—
> Darkness must fly,—
> Where saith the Light of Light,
> "Peace! It is I!"

> *Jesu, Deliverer!*
> *Come thou to me.*
> *Soothe thou my voyaging*
> *Over life's sea!*
> *Thou, when the storm of death*
> *Roars sweeping by,*
> *Whisper, O Truth of Truth!*
> *"Peace! It is I!"*

At this moment I will not further call your attention to the storm or to the calm, but I beg you to observe the feelings of the disciples about the whole matter. The text says that "the men marvelled, saying, What manner of man is this, that even the winds and the sea obey him!"

God evidently thinks much of His people's inward feelings, for they are recorded here and in many other cases. The report of what these poor fishermen felt is as carefully made as the record of what their Lord and Master said, since this was needful to set forth the intent and purpose of their Lord's utterances. God often regards the external action as a mere husk, but the feeling of His people is the innermost kernel in their life story, and He prizes it. Some men practice introspection so much that they grow at last to make a kind of fetish of their inward feeling. This is wrong. Yet there is an error on the other side in which we cease to make known our feelings and think them to be a matter of no consequence, as if there could be real life without feeling. I will declare faith as much as anyone, but there is no need to depreciate all the other graces, and especially all the emotions, in order to do honor to faith. We may honor the heir and yet see no reason for slaying all the rest of the family royal. We must both feel and believe correctly, and it is sometimes good for us to have a lesson about how to feel toward our Lord Jesus Christ. Though feeling must be secondary to faith, yet it is far from being unimportant.

I shall principally address three feelings toward Christ. First, the men marveled. We will dwell upon that—marveling *at Christ's work*. Secondly, if you will turn to Mark 4:41, you will see that Mark describes the feeling of the men as fearing "exceedingly." That shall be our second head—*awestruck at His presence.* Third, we see them in our text *admiring His person,* for they said, "What manner of man," or, more correctly, "What kind of person is this, that even the winds and the sea obey him!"

Marveling at His Work

May I ask you to indulge for a little while the feeling of wonder. You believe in Jesus Christ, and you are saved. Salvation comes not by wondering but at believing; but now, having been saved, having passed from death unto life, and having been preserved for years upon the sea of life in the midst of many tempests, and at this moment enjoying a great calm and restfulness of spirit, I invite you to marvel. What wonderful things Jesus has done for me! It is in my power, if I choose, to waste my time in reading romances, but I care nothing for them, for my own life is to me more romantic than romance. The story of God's goodness to me is more thrilling than any work of fiction could possibly be. I am speaking to some here who I am sure will join with me in owning that there is a freshness, a novelty, a surprise power about the dealings of God with us that we do not meet with anywhere else. Well do we sing in our hymn—"I need not go abroad for joys. I have a feast at home." We can also add that we need not go abroad for wonders, for we have a perfect museum at home in our own experience. John Bunyan, when he was describing the experience of his pilgrim, said, "Oh, world of wonders! I can say no less." And so it is. The life of the godly man on the God side of it, as he receives grace from Jesus, is a gallery of heavenly art, an exhibition of divine skill and power, a wonderland of mercy.

> *Still has my life new wonders seen*
> *Of lovingkindness rare;*
> *A monument of grace I stand,*
> *Thy goodness to declare.*

Let us think for a minute or two of the parallel between us and these disciples as to wonderment. Consider first that the instantaneous and profound calm was *contrary to nature.* The Galilean lake lies in a deep hollow, much below sea level, and in the sides of the cliffs and hills that shut it in there are valleys and openings that act as funnels, down which blasts of cold air from the mountains often rush suddenly. When the time of a storm is really on, the lake of Galilee is not tossed about like an ordinary open sea but is rent and torn and upheaved and almost hurled out of its bed by down-driving hurricanes and twisting whirlwinds. No sailor knows which way the wind blows except that it blows all directions at once, and particularly downward. As if with a direct down-draught from heaven, it blows the vessel into the water and then, changing its course, lifts it into the air. Any mariner who is not used to that strange, wild sea would soon lose his composure and despair of life. It is like a boiling cauldron; the spirits of the vast deep stir it to its bottom, yet this billowy lake in a moment was turned to glass by the word of Jesus: a fact far more wonderful to witness than to read about. Such a change in the uproarious elements was altogether contrary to nature, and therefore "the men marveled."

Now, beloved, look back upon what your life has been. I do not know exactly where you begin your life story. Some commence in the slime pits of Sodom, in vice and drunkenness; others begin with wandering on the dark mountains of infidelity or among the bogs and sloughs of pharisaism and formality. However, it is a miracle that you should have been made to fall at Jesus' feet and cry out for mercy through His precious blood. That you should give up all trust and confidence in self, and at the same time should turn away from favorite lusts that you once reveled in, is such a wonder that nobody would have believed it had it been prophesied to them. Certainly you never would have believed it yourself, and yet it has taken place, and other unlooked-for changes have followed it. Why, you have lived since then in a way that would have been once condemned by yourself as utterly absurd! Had an oracle informed you of it, you would have ridiculed its forecast. "No," you would have said, "I shall never be *that*. I shall never feel *that*. I shall never do *that*."

And yet, so it has been with you. The boiling cauldron of your nature has been cooled down and quieted, and an obedient calm has succeeded rebellious rage. Is it not so? I can only say that if your faith has never produced a wonder, I wonder that you believe in it. If there is not something about you through divine grace that quite surprises your own self, I should not be amazed if one of these days you wake up and find that you have been self-deceived. Far above nature are the ways of grace in men, and if you know them, they have produced in you what your natural temperament and your worldly surroundings never could have produced. There has been fire where you looked for snow and cool streams where you expected flames. A growth of good wheat has been seen where nature would have produced nothing but thorns and briars. Where sin abounded, grace has much more abounded, and your life has become the theater of miracles and the home of wonder.

These men marveled, next, because the calm was so *unexpected by reason*. The ship was nearly going to pieces. A gust of wind threatened to lift her right out of the water, and the next threatened to plunge her to the bottom of the sea. The weary fishers certainly did not look for a calm. When they said, "Master, we perish," I do not know what they thought their Lord would do, but they assuredly never dreamed that He would stand up and say, "Winds and waves, what mean ye? Your Master is here. Be still." That was beyond their nautical experience, and their fathers had never seen such wonders in their day. They could not hope that in a moment they should be in a profound calm.

May I now ask you to wonder a little at what the Lord has done for you? Has He not done for you what you never expected? To speak for myself, I never expected to preach to thousands of God's people. When I was first brought to Jesus, I had no such hope. Why should I be taken from the school and from the desk to lead a part of His flock? I wonder more and more that by His grace I am what I am.

Some of you, when you come to the communion table, may well feel that the most wonderful thing about it is that *you* should find a welcome place at the Lord's own festival. Why, you can hardly tell the way by which the Lord has led you to be a lover of the gospel. Look at your inner feelings as well as your outward position. Are you not often made the subject of desires, of longings, of groanings, and, on the other hand, of enjoyments, of sweet and precious endearments, of high and gracious expectations that utterly surprise you as you remember what you used to be? Are you not "like them that dream" when you think over the Lord's lovingkindness? And if others say that "the Lord has done great things for you," does not your heart chime in with all its bells and ring out the joy notes: "The LORD hath done great things for us, whereof we are glad" (Ps. 126:3)? Come, indulge your wonder. Admire and marvel at the exceeding grace of God toward you in working contrary to nature and contrary to all reasonable expectations and bringing you to be His dear and favored child. Marvels of mercy, wonders of grace, belong to God Most High.

Besides this, the idea of a storm that should immediately be followed by a great calm was *strikingly new to experience*. These fishermen of the Galilean lake had never seen it after this manner before. We read in the Old Testament of some, to whom it was said, "Ye have not passed this way heretofore" (Josh. 3:4). Certainly the same might have been said to these disciples: "You have been in a tempest, but never in your lives before were you one minute in a tempest and the next in a calm." It must have been enough to make them weep for joy or, at least, it must have led them to hold up their hands in glad astonishment. The deliverance wrought by their Lord was so fresh, so altogether new, that marveling was natural.

Have you not often experienced that which has astounded you by its novelty? Are not God's mercies new every morning? I address some of you who have been forty or fifty years in the ways of God: do you not find a continual freshness in the manifestations of God's goodness to you both in providence and in grace? Let me ask you, has spiritual life been to you like mounting a treadmill—monotonous, wearisome, uniform? If so, there is something wrong with you, for while we live near to God, we dwell under new heavens and walk upon a new earth. When a man travels through the Alps on a bright sunshiny day, all things are as though born that morning: that drop of dew on the grass he never saw before; that drifting cloud has newly arrived upon the scene. Never before has the traveler seen the face of nature radiant with the same smile as that which now delights him. Has it not been so with you in the journey of life? Have not all things become new and remained new since you were born anew? Has not grace been heaped upon grace, so that each new experience has excelled its predecessor?

Still have I beheld fresh beauties in my Master's face, fresh glories in my Master's Word, fresh assurance of His faithfulness in His providence, fresh power in my Master's Spirit as He has dealt graciously with my soul. I know that it is so with you, and I want you to marvel at it that God should devise a thousand things most rare and new for such insignificant people as we are. Glory be to His blessed Name. It may well be said of us, "The men marveled and said, 'What manner of person is this who dealeth so with His people?'" Who is a God like unto Thee? What is man that Thou art mindful of him? And the son of man that Thou visitest him? These three things made the disciples wonder.

There was another. I should think that it was a great marvel to them that a calm was sent *so soon* after the storm. Man needs time, but God's *Word* runs very quickly. Man travels with weary steps, but the Lord rides upon a cherub and flies upon the wings of the wind. The particles of air and the drops of water were all in confusion through the tempest, rushing as if chaos had come again, rising in whirlwinds and falling in cataracts, yet they did but see the face of their Maker, and they were still. In one single instant there was a calm. Have not you and I experienced instantaneous workings of divine grace upon our spirits? It may not be so with all, but some of us at the first instant of our faith lost the burden of sin in a moment. Our load was all gone before we knew where we were. The change from sorrow to joy was not worked in us by degrees, but in a moment, the sun leaped above the horizon and the night of our soul was over. Has it not been so since? We have been in the midst of God's people with a heavy spirit and without power to enjoy a truth or to perform a holy act. The hymns seemed a mockery and the prayer an empty form, and yet in a single moment, the rod of the Lord has touched the rock and the waters have flowed forth, and by the very means of grace that seemed so dull and powerless, we have been enlivened and comforted.

We have blessed the Lord that ever we came to the place. I do not know how it is that we undergo such sudden changes. Yes I do. It is because God works all good things in us, and He is able to accomplish in an instant that which we could not effect in a year. He can in a moment change our prison into a palace and our ashes into beauty. He can bid us put off our sackcloth and put on the wedding garments of delight. As in the twinkling of an eye, this corruptible shall put on incorruption, so in an instant our spiritual death can blossom into heavenly life. This is a great wonder. Go and marvel at what the Lord has so speedily done for you.

And then to think that it should have been *so perfect*. When a storm subsides, the sea is generally angry for hours, if not for days. A great wind at Dover can make the English Channel rough for some time. But when our Lord Jesus makes a calm, the sea forgets her raging and smiles at once. In fact, "He maketh the storm a calm, so that the waves thereof are still" (Ps. 107:29). The winds hush all their fury and are quiet in an instant when He bids them rest. And oh, when the Lord gives joy and peace and blessedness to His people, He does not do it by halves. "When he giveth quietness, who then can make trouble?" (Job 34:29). There is no such thing as a half blessing for a child of God. The Lord gives him fullness of peace— "the peace of God, which passeth all understanding" (Phil. 4:7). He causes him to enjoy quiet through believing, and He enables him to rejoice in tribulation also, for tribulation works blessing to the souls of men.

I cannot write as much as I could wish, but I shall finish this division of the discourse by saying that one point of wonder was that the calm was *wrought so evidently by the Master's Word*. He spoke, and it was done. His will was revealed in a word, and that will was law. Not an atom of matter dares to move if the divine fiat forbids. The sovereignty of Jesus is supreme, and His Word is with power.

Now, dear friend, I know that there must have been very much that is wonderful in your life as a Christian. But do not think yourself the only partaker of such wonderment. Let us all sit down and inquire of each other, "Why me, Lord? How can such great grace be shown to me. How can the Son of God stoop to look at me and take me into marriage union with Himself, promise that I shall live because He lives, that I shall reign because He reigns?" Sit down, I say, and believingly marvel, and marvel, and marvel, and never leave off marveling. And let me drop one little word into your ear. Is there something that you desire of God concerning which unbelief has said that it is too wonderful to be expected? Let that be the reason why you shall expect it. There is nothing to a Christian so probable as the unexpected, and there is nothing that God is so likely to do for us as that which is above all we ask or even think.

God is at home in wonderland. If what you want is an ordinary thing, perhaps it may not come, but if it strikes you as a marvel, you are in a ready state of heart to honor God for it, and you are likely to receive it. Do not think that because between you and heaven there will be a giant's causeway of marvels, you will never get there. On the contrary, conclude that the God who began to save you by so great a miracle as the gift and death of His own dear Son will go on to perfect salvation even if He has to fling into the sea a thousand heavens to make stepping-stones for you to tread upon before you can reach His presence. "He that spared not his own Son, but delivered him up for us all, how shall he not with him also freely give us all things?" (Rom. 8:32). Therefore expect wonders. These men marveled: expect to keep on marveling till you get to heaven and to keep on marveling when you are in heaven, and throughout eternity. Wonder will be a principal ingredient of our adoration in heaven.

Awestruck at Our Lord's Presence

Mark says that "the men feared greatly." They feared greatly because they found themselves in the presence of One who had stilled the winds and the waves. It is good to cultivate that holy familiarity that comes from nearness to Jesus, and yet we ought always to be humbled by a sense of that nearness. Permit me to remind the boldest believer that our loving Lord is still God over all. He is to be honored and reverenced, worshiped and adored, by all who draw near to Him. However much He is our brother, He says, "Ye call me Master and Lord: and ye say well; for so I am" (John 13:13). He is all the greater because of His condescension to us, as we are bound to recognize this.

Whenever Jesus is near, the feeling of holy awe and solemn dread will steal over true disciples. I am afraid of that way of being so familiar with Christ as to talk of Him as "dear Jesus" and "dear Lord," as if He were some Jack or Harry that we might pat on the back whenever we liked. No, no. This will never do. It is not such language as men would use to their prince; let them not thus address the King of kings. However favored we may be, we are but dust and ashes, and our spirit must be chastened with reverence.

When Jesus is near, we should fear exceedingly *because we have doubted Him.* If you had been suspicious of a dear friend and had indulged hard thoughts about him, and suddenly you found yourself sitting in the same room with him, you would feel awkward, especially if you understood that he knew what you had said and thought. You will feel ashamed of yourself if Jesus shall draw near to you. The wisest thing you can do in such a case is to say, "My Master, my Lord, since You favor me with Your presence, I will first fall at Your feet and confess that I did doubt You, that I did think that the stormy wind would swallow up the vessel, and that the waves would devour both You and me. Forgive me, Master, forgive me for having thought so little of You." Whenever we are near to Christ, one of the first feelings should be that of great humiliation. Let us fall at His feet.

We have been so foolish as to fear His creatures, paying to them a sort of worship of fear, as if they had more power to harm than Jesus had to help. We clothe wind and sea with attributes that belong to God only. We look upon our trials as if they tried the Lord, too, and vanquished Him because they vanquish us. Are we not because of this smitten with dread in the presence of the Christ?

The next feeling should be—since He has come to me, this Mighty One who has worked such marvels for me—*let me try to order myself aright in His presence.* I notice whenever the Lord Jesus Christ is very present in our congregation how carefully everybody sings. I notice about tune, time, and a tone difference from the singing that is usual, an acquired skill in music. Though it may seem a trifle, yet I cannot help observing that when people come to the communion table as a matter of routine, they frequently behave roughly, walking noisily and looking about, or else they sit like statues, with a cold propriety of posture and vacancy of countenance. But you will notice that fellowship with Jesus affects the glance of the eye, the thoughts of the soul, and consequently the movements of the body. When a man is truly conscious that Jesus, the Wonder-worker, is near, he fears exceedingly. If ever you say to Jesus, "You know that I love You," mind you put "Lord" before it— "Lord, You know all things," for He is your Lord still.

Where Jesus is there is godly fear, which is by no means the same as slavish fear. Every true child has a reverence for his father. Every true daughter has a loving respect for her mother. So it is with us toward our Lord Jesus. We owe so much to Him, and He is so great and so good, and we are so little and so sinful, that there must be a blessed sense of holy awe whenever we come before Him. Indulge it. Indulge it now. You know how John puts it: "When I saw him, I fell at his feet as dead" (Rev. 1:17). Why, that is the man who leaned his head on the bosom of Christ. Yes, that is the man who fell at His feet as dead. If your head has never leaned upon the bosom of the Lord, I should not wonder whether you can hold it up in His presence. But when it has once lain there in con-fiding love, reposing upon boundless mercy, then that head of yours will lie in the dust uncrowned if God has honored it. It will be your delight to cast your crown at His feet and give Him all the glory. Reign forever, King of kings and Lord of lords! Conquer me, my Lord. Subdue me perfectly. Make dust of me beneath Your feet, if You shall be but the tenth of an inch the higher for my down-casting. O my Master and my Lord, with joy I would shrink to nothing before You that You may be all in all. May this be your feel-ing and mine. The men feared exceedingly; let us fear also, after a believing sort.

Admiring the Person of Jesus

These men who marveled and who feared exceedingly admired the person of Him who had set them free from the storm, saying, "What manner of person is this, that even the wind and the sea obey him?" Come, let us admire and adore the nature of Christ that is altogether beyond our comprehension. The winds and the sea obeyed Him, though He had slept like other men. When His head was that of an infant, the crown of the universe was about His brow. When He was in the carpenter's shop, He was still the

Creator of all worlds. When He went to die upon the tree, a myriad of angels would have come to rescue Him if He had but willed it. Even in His humiliation, He was still the Son of the Highest, God over all, blessed for ever. Now that He is exalted in heaven, do not forget the other side of the question; believe that He is just as much man as when He was here—as truly a brother of our race as He is God over all, blessed forevermore.

Let us now give our hearts to admiration of Him in *His complex nature that is beyond comprehension.* He is my next of kin, and yet my God; at once my Redeemer and my Lord. We may each one cry with Job, "I know that my redeemer liveth, and that he shall stand at the latter day upon the earth; And though after my skin worms destroy this body, yet in my flesh shall I see God" (Job 19:25–26). Because He lives as my kinsman, there is the sweetness of it; and because He is my God, there is the glory of it. He is both tenderly compassionate for my infirmities and gloriously able to overcome them. He is a complete Savior because He is both human and divine. Come, my soul, bow down in wonder that ever God should send such a Savior as this to you. There is one Savior, the Son of man and yet the mighty God, and He cannot be moved. Joy then and rejoice in the nature of your blessed Lord.

Next, rejoice in *His power that has no limit,* so that even the winds and the waves obey Him. The winds—can they have a master? The waves that cast their spray upon the face of princes—can they own a sovereign? Yes, the most fickle of elements, the most unruly of forces, are all under the power of Jesus. Joy and rejoice in this. Little as well as great—Atlantic that divides the world and that little drop in the basin of Gennesaret—are alike in the hand of Jesus. The power of God is seen in a falling mountain when it crushes a village, but it is as truly present when a rose leaf falls upon the garden walk. God is seen when an angel dashes from heaven to earth, and is He not seen when a bee flits from flower to flower? Jesus is the master of the little as well as of the great, yea, King of all things.

I joy this moment to think that even the wicked actions of ungodly men, though they are not deprived of their sinfulness, so as to make the men the less responsible, are nevertheless overruled by that great Lord of ours, who works all things according to the counsel of His will. In the front I see Jesus leading the van of providence. Behind He guards the rear. On the heights I see Jesus reigning King of kings and Lord of lords. In the deeps I mark the terror of His justice as He binds the dragon with his chain. Let the universal cry of "Hallelujah" rise to the Son of God, world without end.

Sit down and admire and adore His unlimited power and then conclude by paying homage to *that sovereignty of His that tolerates no question*. Notice that not only did the winds and waves perform His will, but also, as if they were waking into life and rising into intelligent knowledge of Him, they are said to *obey* Him. I gather not only that Christ is the forceful master of unintelligent agencies but also that He is the sovereign master of things that can obey Him; and He will be obeyed. Ah, you may bite and hiss at Him, but as the viper broke his teeth against the file yet hurt it not, so shall the ungodly exercise all their craft and all their strength, and the end shall be shame and confusion of face to them. The kingdom of our Lord and Master is by some thought to be a long way off, and His cause is half despaired of by fainthearted men; but He who sits in the heavens laughs at the impatience of saints as well as at the impiety of sinners, for He knows that all is well. Out of seeming evil He produces good, and from that good a better still, and better still in infinite progression.

All things move toward His eternal coronation. As once every atom of history converged to His cross; so does it today project itself towards His crown. The Lord Jesus comes to His well-earned throne as surely as He came to the shameful cross. He comes, and when He comes it shall be as when He rose in the ship and rebuked the winds and the men marveled. All storms of raging passion, conflicting opinion, and fierce warfare shall be hushed, and He shall be admired in His saints and glorified in all them who believe. Even unbelievers shall marvel at Him and say, "What manner of person is this, that even earth and hell obey Him, and all things are subjected to His sovereign power!"

Happy are the eyes that shall see Him in that day with joy. Happy are the men who shall sit at the right hand of the Coming One. O beloved, your eyes and mine shall see it if we have first looked to the Redeemer upon the cross and found salvation in Him. Courage, brethren. Let the waves dash and the winds howl. The Lord of hosts is with us. The God of Jacob is our refuge. All is safe because of His presence, and all shall end gloriously because of His manifestation. The Lord bless you, in tempest and in calm, for Christ's sake.

I ask you, does there exist in this world a greater nuisance than yourself? I know you will say, "No, there may be other filthy and abominable things, but I feel myself to be the most loathsome incarnation of filthiness that ever could have existed. I did not always think myself to be so, but I do now. I do not simply feel that I am dead and powerless, but I feel offensive to myself, so that I wish I could run away from myself. I feel offensive, moreover, to God, utterly obnoxious to Him." Well, then, if that is your feeling, you are brought low enough, for it is just when we begin to corrupt, as the body of Lazarus did, and we, like Martha, are for giving everything up as hopeless, that Jesus Christ calls as He did then, "Lazarus, come forth."

Chapter Eleven

The Spiritual Resurrection

And when he thus had spoken, he cried with a loud voice,
Lazarus, come forth. And he that was dead came forth, bound
hand and foot with graveclothes: and his face was bound about
with a napkin. Jesus saith unto them, Loose him, and let him go.
—John 11:43–44.

PERHAPS THE LEGITIMATE TOPIC of this chapter should be the resurrection of the dead. Lazarus had died and was lying in his grave. At the invitation of his sisters, Jesus Christ came to see them, and His visit answered the double purpose of comforting the bereaved and restoring the dead. It would be a blessed and an excellent topic were we to enlarge upon the wonders of the resurrection. We shall do so for a few moments, and then we shall come to the principal theme that concerns the spiritual resurrection from a spiritual death.

The very fact that Lazarus came from his grave after he had lain there four days and was corrupt and that he was called from the sepulchre by the mighty voice of Jesus is to us a proof that the dead shall rise at the voice of Jesus at the last great day. Every Christian believes that there is to be a resurrection of the dead. But unfortunately, the great doctrine of the resurrection is not emphasized by most as it should be. In early times, the resurrection was preached by the apostles as being the sum and substance of the gospel. Wherever Paul went, we know that he spoke concerning the resurrection of the dead; and then, "some mocked" (Acts 17:32). But now if we speak concerning the after-state of the departed, we generally emphasize the aspect of immortality, not of resurrection. Yet, immortality was known to the ancients before the gospel came. They believed in a kind of immortality, but resurrection never entered into the thoughts of the heathen. Many of them believed in the immortality of the soul. Those who had been enlightened by powerful reason or remnants of ancient tradition believed that the soul did not die but lived on in a future state.

But the immortality of the soul is very different from the Christian doctrine of the resurrection of the body. We believe that the soul is immortal and shall last forever, but we believe something more than that. We believe that the body is immortal, too, and that after this body shall have been lain in the grave, in the Lord's good time it shall be raised again. It shall either be translated to heaven, there to enjoy bliss eternally, or be sent down to hell, to suffer forever and ever.

The doctrine of the resurrection of the dead belongs peculiarly to Christianity. It was never taught by any rationalists or philosophers. They might hold the transmigration of souls, but the resurrection of the body they did not hold. But we, as Christians, do really believe that this body that we now inhabit, though it must die and see corruption, shall be raised again from the dust. We believe that whatever you do with the body—divide it, scatter it, burn it—God, by the fiat of His omnipotence, shall rebuild the fabric to become the habitation of the living soul forever and ever. We dare not deny this, because we are expressly taught it in the sacred writings and it has been so fully and satisfactorily proved by the apostle Paul.

Is it not a blessed fact that we shall rise again? I see among my church some whose countenance tells me that they have lost a friend or mother or a father. Others, I know, have laid beloved infants in the dust. Others have had a precious husband or wife taken from them. Ah, despair not, you who mourn! Here is a fact for you—not only that your soul and the soul of your loved one shall meet in eternity but also that the same body on which you doted shall, if you are believers, be seen by you in heaven. The eyes of the tender and pious mother who once dropped tears on you shall behold you in heaven, and the hand of that pious father, now lying in the grave, that once lay on your head and consecrated you to the Lord shall be grasped by you in heaven. Not only shall the soul of that infant live forever and ever, but its beautiful body that contained the soul of your child shall live again. It shall not be a fictitious resurrection. It shall not be a new race of ethereal creatures, but actual bodies shall be ours.

If you have been bereft of all your friends—if they have departed in the faith of Jesus—you shall see them again! "Blessed are the dead which die in the Lord from henceforth: Yea, saith the Spirit, that they may rest from their labours; and their works do follow them" (Rev. 14:13). But yet more blessed are they to be: "for the trumpet shall sound, and the dead shall be raised incorruptible" (1 Cor. 15:52), and we shall see the bodies of those we once loved on earth. Those bodies we once silently gazed upon, as they lay in all the stiffness of death, we shall see quickened and glorified. The mortal shall "put on immortality," and corruptible shall "put on incorruption." It was "sown in weakness," and we wept when we saw it lowered into the grave, but it shall be "raised in power" (1 Cor. 15:43). It was "sown a natural body," and though it shall be "raised a spiritual body" (1 Cor. 15:44), yet it shall be a body to all intents and purposes, as it was before, and we shall recognize it as such.

Ah, beloved! Does not this make Christianity worth having? Does not this light up the grave with a supernatural splendor—this glorious, this overpowering, this more than natural, this superhuman doctrine of the resurrection of the dead? I will not stop to picture the scene. I might tell you of the silent graves and of the church-yards covered with the grass of ages. I might picture to you the battlefield. I might bid you hear the voice of Jesus when, descending with the sound of the trumpet and with an exceeding great army of angels, He shall say, "Awake, you dead, and come to judgment!" When He cries, "Awake!" eyes that have been glazed for many a year shall open, bodies that have long been stiffened shall regain their energy and stand upright. Not sheeted ghosts, not phantoms, not visions, but actual beings shall rise—the same persons who were buried. I see them bursting the cerements of the grave, dashing open their coffin lids, and coming forth. Ah, we shall see them, and each one for himself shall rise! There shall rise Lazarus, and Martha, and Mary; and loved ones that belong to us, whom long we have wept as departed, we shall then rejoice over as having been recovered.

So much by way of preliminary remarks concerning the resurrection from the dead. Now let us deal with the subject in another manner. The death of Lazarus, his burial in the tomb, and his corruption are a figure and picture of the spiritual condition of every soul by nature. The voice of Jesus, crying, "Lazarus, come forth," is an emblem of the voice of Jesus, by His Spirit that quickens the soul. And the fact that Lazarus, even when alive, wore his graveclothes for a little while, until they were taken from him, is extremely significant. If we allegorize upon it, it teaches us that even when a soul is quickened into spiritual life, it still wears some of its graveclothes, which are only torn off when Jesus afterward says, "Loose him, and let him go."

We propose, therefore, to consider these three points: *the slumber of death*, in which every soul lies by nature. Second, we will hear *the voice of life*; "Jesus cried with a loud voice, Lazarus, come forth." And third, we will note *the partial bondage* that even the living soul has to endure, which is emblematized by Lazarus' coming forth bound hand and foot and having his face wrapped about with a napkin.

The Slumber of Death

Come with me now, Christian, to "the rock whence ye are hewn, and to the hole of the pit whence ye are digged" (Isa. 51:1). Come with me to the house of death, for there your soul once lay, "dead in trespasses and sins" (Eph. 2:1). There are some in this world, we know, who utterly deny that the sinner is really dead in sins. I remember hearing a preacher assert that though the Scriptures said that men were dead, they meant only metaphorically so. I always like, when there is a metaphor, to keep the metaphor. Some of the eminent doctors in Rowland Hill's day said that there were no such beings as angels, that they were only Oriental metaphors. "Very well," said Rowland Hill, "then it was a company of Oriental metaphors that sang at the birth of Christ, 'Glory to God in the highest.' Then it was an Oriental metaphor that slew 185,000 of Sennacherib's army in a single night. It was an Oriental metaphor that appeared to Peter in prison, that knocked off his chains, and led him through the streets. Truly," said he, "these Oriental metaphors are wonderful things!"

I will try the same rule here. "You hath he metaphorically quickened, who were metaphorically dead in trespasses and sins!" A fine metaphorical gospel that is! Then again: "To be carnally minded, is metaphorical death; but to be spiritually minded, is metaphorical life and peace." Such language does not mean anything at all. My friends, it is all nonsense about metaphorical death; men are *really* dead in a spiritual sense.

But I must tell you what this death constitutes. There are different grades of life: understand that to commence with. There is life in a plant that a stone does not possess; therefore, a stone is dead. There is life in an animal that the plant does not possess. Then again, there is soulish life; and since the animal has no soul, you might say that the animal is soully dead. Then there is a grade beyond the soulish life of a man—a spiritual life. To an ungodly man, there are only two parts—soul and body. To the Christian, there are three—body, soul, and *spirit*. And as a body without a soul would be dead naturally, so a man without a spirit—a man who has not had a spark struck off from the great orb of light called God—is spiritually dead. Nevertheless, there are some who assert that men who are ungodly are spiritually alive. If you think this, I must argue with you a little while.

First of all, if you are spiritually alive and can do spiritual actions, the first thing I ask you is, *Why do you not do them now?* Some men say that they can repent and believe when they like, and they do not believe that to do this, they need the power of the Spirit. Then, sir, if you can do it, and do not do it, if any man deserves to be damned, it is you.

The next thing I have to say is this. You say, "I am not dead; I have spiritual life and can pray and repent and believe." Let me ask, *Have you tried to do it?* Do you say yes? Well, then, I know you will confess, unless you will lie before God, that you have found out your inability. There never was a man yet who strived to pray sincerely before God but he felt something repressing his devotion. When he has come before God, under an agony of guilt, crying out for mercy, he has felt at times as if he could not pray, as if he could not utter a single word. Have you known what it is to be in such a condition that you cannot pray, that you cannot believe, that you cannot repent. Have you put your hand on your heart and said, "O God, my heart is hard! I wish it would melt. I cannot break it"? When you would pray, do you not feel that your heart is far away, wandering in the world?

The best method of proving a man's inability is to set him about doing the thing. When the young man said, "All these things have I kept from my youth up," Jesus said, "Go and sell that thou hast" (Matt. 19:20–21). Ah, beloved, when God brought us to Himself, we wrestled in prayer and pleaded with Him. But we were taught, after all, that the power for everything spiritual must come from God, for there were certain times and seasons when we could not more have prayed than we could have flown up to heaven, when we could no more have believed than we could have taken the moon in our hands. We could not grasp a promise; we could not grapple with a single temptation; we felt ourselves to be powerless, lost, dead. Sinner! I tell you that you are dead as to all spiritual matters, and dead you ever will be if left to yourself. The sovereign will and power of God alone must give you life, or else you can do nothing except sin. Neither righteous acts nor coming to Jesus can you ever do of yourself.

But I hear someone say, "*If I cannot do anything, I will sit down where I am and make myself content.*" What, will you sit down, when hell blazes before you, when the pit is yawning at your feet, when damnation stares you in the face, when God is angry with you, when your sins are bellowing out to high heaven for condemnation? Will you sit down? As well might a man sit on yonder housetop when the flames are rising around him; as well might he float down the rapids to be at once dashed to pieces. If you talk about sitting down, you give me the best proof in all the world that you are "dead in trespasses and sins." For if you were not dead, you would be crying out, "O God, quicken me! O God, give me life! I know that I am dead. I feel that I can do nothing, but You have promised to do it all for me. Though I am less than nothing, You have omnipotence to give me life."

Do you not see that I am putting you down that Christ may pick you up? Do you not see that I am laying you low, not to perish, not to be trampled on in the dust, but rather that, like a corn of wheat, you might fall into the ground and die and afterward be quickened and bring forth fruit? For nothing can bring a man into a state of life so well as a feeling of death. And if I could get my readers, one and all, to recognize, acknowledge, and feel that they were in a state of spiritual death and utterly powerless, I could then have hope for them. For no man can confess himself to be dead and yet sit down contentedly. He will cry out for grace and ask God to deliver him from that death.

I have yet to tell you that *the ungodly man is something more than dead.* He is like Lazarus lying in his tomb. You remember those plain words that Martha spoke to Jesus. They are translated into simple English, and I daresay the Hebrew is quite as expressive: "Lord, by this time he stinketh: for he hath been dead four days" (John 11:39). Ay, and this is the condition of every ungodly man. Not only is he dead, but he is positively corrupt in God's sight. There are those who know what I mean when I say they not only groan under a sense of spiritual death but also feel themselves to be a stench in their own nostrils and in God's also.

I ask you, does there exist in this world a greater nuisance than yourself? I know you will say, "No, there may be other filthy and abominable things, but I feel myself to be the most loathsome incarnation of filthiness that ever could have existed. I did not always think myself to be so, but I do now. I do not simply feel that I am dead and powerless, but I feel offensive to myself, so that I wish I could run away from myself. I feel offensive, moreover, to God, utterly obnoxious to Him." Well, then, if that is your feeling, you are brought low enough, for it is just when we begin to corrupt, as the body of Lazarus did, and we, like Martha, are for giving everything up as hopeless, that Jesus Christ calls as He did then, "Lazarus, come forth."

The Voice of Life

We commence, then, with this wonder-working process by saying that *the giving of life to Lazarus was instantaneous.* There lay Lazarus in the grave—dead and corrupt. Jesus cried aloud, "Lazarus, come forth." We do not read that a single moment elapsed between the time when Christ said the word and when Lazarus came out of his grave. It did not take the soul an instant to wing its way from Hades into the body of Lazarus, nor did that body need any delay to become alive again. So, if the Lord speaks to a man and quickens him to spiritual life, it is an instantaneous work. If the Lord speaks to you, life will come into you in a moment, in one single instant. The power of grace is shown in this, that it converts a man instantly. It does not take hours to justify—justification is done in a moment; it does not take hours to regenerate—regeneration is done in a second. We are born, and we die, naturally, in instants, and so it is with regard to spiritual death and spiritual life. They occupy no period of time but are done instantly whenever Jesus speaks. If my Master would cry, "Lazarus, come forth," there is not a Lazarus who is reading—although covered with the shroud of drunkenness, bound about with a belt of swearing, or surrounded with a huge coffin of evil habit and wickedness—who would not burst that coffin and come forth a living man.

But mark, *it was not the disciples, but Jesus, who said, "Lazarus, come forth."* How often have I strived to preach my congregation, if possible, into life, but that could not be done. I remember times when my whole soul has agonized over men, every nerve of my body has been strained, and I could have wept my very being out of my eyes and carried my whole frame away in a flood of tears if I could but win souls. On such occasions, we preach as if we had men before us personally and were clutching them and begging them to come to Christ! But with all that, I know I never made a soul alive yet and never shall. I am perfectly conscious that all the pleadings of all the living ambassadors from God will never induce a sinner to come to Jesus unless Jesus comes to that sinner. Peter might have cried for a long while, "Lazarus, come forth," before Lazarus would have moved an inch. So might James or John. But when Jesus does it, it is done to purpose. Does not this lower the pride of the minister? What is he? He is a poor little trumpet through which God blows, but nothing else. In vain do I scatter seed; it is upon God the harvest depends. All my brethren in the ministry might preach till they were blind, but they would have no success unless the Spirit attended the quickening Word.

But though the hearer cannot do it and although the minister cannot do it, I want to persuade you, if I can, that *dead as you are, Jesus can speak you to life.* Let me single out a character, for I like to do that. There is a man who says, "I have been living fifty years in sin and am worse than ever. My old habits bind me hand and foot, and I have no hope of being delivered." Now, if Jesus says, "Lazarus, come forth," you will come forth in an instant. "Nay, but," you say "I am corrupt." Ah, but Christ is mightier than your corruption! Do you say, "I am dead"? Nay, but Christ is "life." Do you say, "I am bound hand and foot and in a dungeon of darkness?" Nay, but Christ is a light in darkness, and He will disperse the gloom. You say, perhaps, "I do not deserve it," but Jesus cares nothing for deserving. The dead body of Lazarus deserved nothing; it was putrid and only deserved to have the stone covering it forever. "Roll away the stone," says Christ; and oh, what an offensive smell issues forth! And you may be one for whom Jesus Christ has rolled away the stone right now. You may be standing at your own grave feeling loathsome and offensive. But still, offensive as you are, Jesus asks no merit of you. He will give you His merits. It is only for Him to say, "Come forth," and you will come forth from your grave and be made alive in Christ Jesus. May our God wake our dead souls and bring them to life by His summons, "Lazarus, come forth."

Yet I hear another person saying, "But I am afraid, sir, that if I were told to come forth, the devil would not let me. He has been oppressing me so long. He has been trying to keep me down and to make me lie still in my grave. I feel that he is now sitting upon my breast and weighing down all my hopes and quenching all my love." But let me tell you, there is not one down in hell that is so mighty as Christ is in heaven. The evil one is in Christ's power, and if you will but call upon Him, if He has enabled you only to utter a groan, He will cry unto you, "Come forth," and you shall live.

The Partial Bondage

Even when a soul is called by divine grace from death to life, yet it often wears its graveclothes for a long while. Many of my dear friends are afraid they are not converted, because they do not have as much faith and assurance and do not know as much as others. So they are afraid they are not alive. I have a word of comfort for them. The fact that Lazarus came forth in his graveclothes, with a napkin wrapped about his head, teaches us that many of us, though we are alive in Christ, still have our graveclothes on. Many believers still are not quite free from trusting in works. They have not yet come to believe that salvation is by sovereign grace alone and will not have some works mixed up with it. They fear that, after all, God may cast them out of the covenant. Oh, if we could but tear their napkin off! We will not quarrel with them, we will not be angry with them; but we think we hear Jesus Christ say to us, "Loose them, and let them go."

This, however, is not the point I want to dwell on with you, because I think most of you have got that napkin off your eyes. But *when we first obtain spiritual life, how many graveclothes there are hanging about us!* A man who has been a drunkard, even though he becomes a living child of God, will sometimes find his old habits clinging to him. I have known many drunkards give up their drunkenness, but when they have been going by a tavern, they have thought that for the life of them, they could not keep from going in. And they have often well nigh gone astray, and their feet have almost slipped. And the man who has been a swearer will confess that there have been times when the vile words have almost come from his lips—perhaps not quite—I hope not, but there will be enough to show that he has some of his graveclothes still hanging about him. We have known men who have indulged in other kinds of vices and sins, and whenever an opportunity has presented itself, there has been the old feeling getting up and saying, "Let me do it, let me do it." And they have strived to keep it down, but they have hardly been strong enough.

Those graveclothes will keep on very tightly until the habit is quite broken off. I believe there is not a Christian living who has not some shreds of his graveclothes remaining. Until we lie down in the grave, I believe we shall carry them with us. Look at poor Paul; who could have been a more holy man than he? Yet he cried, "O wretched man that I am! who shall deliver me from the body of this death?" (Rom. 7:24). Let this comfort and cheer the man who has come to Christ but who is yet striving against his corruption. Perhaps his unbelief says, "If you were a child of God, you would not have these wicked thoughts and inclinations." But let me ask, do you hate those thoughts and inclinations? Then tell the devil next time that he assails you thus, that he lies, for verily, this is not a sign that you are not the Lord's, but rather a sign that you are His. For if you were not a child of God, you would not mind these things, but since you are His child, you strive against them.

These wicked graveclothes will show themselves sometimes. I know some who seem as if they could not get rid of their old angry tempers as long as they live. Their graveclothes have been rent in shreds by divine grace, but the shreds hang about them still. Do not think I am speaking to exonerate or excuse you, but I am striving to comfort you. You may be spiritually alive with these graveclothes on if you struggle against them and try to get them off. But if you love them, they are not your graveclothes but are your living clothes; you are doing the work of your father, and his wages you shall have. If you feel your sins to be graveclothes and are anxious to get rid of them, though you cannot conquer all your sins and corruptions, be not dismayed. Trust in Christ. Though the graveclothes yet hang about you, still trust His mercy and His grace, for by and by Jesus Christ shall say, "Loose him, and let him go."

We are loosed first from one bad habit and then from another. All the while I live, I feel that I carry some of my graveclothes about me—the garment that encumbers me and the sin that does most easily beset me. But by and by, the time will come, and Christ will say, "Loose him, and let him go." I see one lying on his bed, the eye glancing upward to heaven, the pulses faint and few, the breath drawn heavily, the body decaying. What does all this mean? Why, it is the undoing of the wires of the cage. And in a little while, when sickness and pain have done their work, Christ will say, "Loose him, and let him go."

I remember hearing a minister tell of his pious sister's deathbed. When she was very near dying, she said, "Sit me up a moment," and they did. She then said, "Oh! that the final word were given, Loose me, and let me rise to heaven, and wrap myself in God." In a moment or two, she fell back. God had said, "Loose her, and let her go." How our disembodied spirits will rejoice when God says, "Loose them, and let them go." We are fettered now, but we shall be emancipated then. Then our spirits shall fly more rapidly than the flashing lightning; then shall they be wafted along, swifter than the gales of the North or the winds of the South. We shall fly upward to our God and be free forever from all that now distresses us.

And now a thought or two to finish up with. Before God will say, "Loose him, and let him go," recollect, you must have had life. Now I come to this last solemn enquiry: *Do you have this life?* How frequently it is the case that we preach to our people with all our soul and might, and yet nobody takes it home to himself! But I would not let you go, feeble as I am and unable to say much to you, until I have tried to press this matter home upon your soul. In a little while I, too, must stand before God's judgment, and when I think of it, it is enough to make me tremble. When I call to mind the tens and hundreds of thousands unto whom I have ministered the Word of the gospel and think if there should, on the last day, be found one person who shall lay his damnation to my charge, how horrible and terrible must be my lot! If, after having preached to others, I should have been unfaithful and should prove a castaway (1 Cor. 9:27), what an awful thing that would be!

In these days, when it is advertised that there is a special sermon to be preached, people rush off to hear a popular preacher or somebody who happens to be much talked about. But do you know what that man does when he preaches and what you do when you hear? Are you aware that every time that man stands in the pulpit, if he is unfaithful, he subjects himself to the wrath of God? Do you not know that if, at last, that man who stands up to preach to the people should have been discovered to have preached false doctrine, his doom must be horrible in the extreme? And do you recollect that when you hear, it is not as if you go to see a play or to listen to a recital? You are listening to a man who professes to speak by God and for God and to speak for your good, and his heart yearns over you. It is solemn work to preach, and it should be solemn work to hear! For every preaching and every hearing, the Lord will call us to account in the last great day, when He shall judge the secrets of men by Jesus Christ.

So what have I said to you in this message? I have told you, first, that you are dead. You may go away and laugh at it, but laughing at it will not make you alive. I have told you, in the next place, that Christ can make you alive, and yet you may despise that Christ; but your despising Him will not free you from condemnation at the last great day. I have told you of the bands of death that bind you, and yet you are, perhaps, tempted to smile. But if you never sorrow over the bands of death here, you will have to wear clanking fetters forever. Did I speak of fiction when I said that? I speak not of fiction but of a dread reality. There is, somewhere, a place where the fire of Gehenna shall torture bodies forever and where unutterable misery shall pain souls. And oh, tremble, you heavens, and shake, you hills! O earth, let your solid ribs of brass shake and let your bowels be dissolved! It is a fact, and a fearful fact, that there is a hell. I know not where it is—my spirit longs not to visit that dread region—but there are souls there that are biting their bonds of iron and shrieking out under inexpressible torture. And there are some of your friends and relations there, perhaps— some with whom you drained the wine cups, the harlot, the adulterer, the thief, and such-like persons. There they are, in hell, at this hour.

Do you believe it? I do not think you do, but do you believe God's Word? Or are you hardy infidels and deny it? "It *is* true," you say. Then are you so mad and irrational as to persevere in such a road? O sirs, if there were some tremendous precipice and I saw you hastily approaching it, would I not cry out to you and say, "Stop! stop! stop! There is ruin before you!" May I not plead with you for your life, that you may be led to stop your course of sin! For "the wages of sin is death," while "the gift of God is eternal life through Jesus Christ our Lord" (Rom. 6:23), whom you are shunning, avoiding, and grieving. Must I not plead with you? Shall you be going to hell blindfolded, and shall not one of your poor fellow creatures pull the bandage from your eyes? Shall he not call to you without being thought mad or an enthusiast? Well, if I am mad, in that respect, may I ever be so. And if that is to be an enthusiast, let none be sober! But if it is mad and enthusiastic to go to heaven, how much more so it is to go to hell!

Do you ask me to tell you that before I finish? Do I hear one say, "What must I do to be saved?" I answer, "Believe on the Lord Jesus Christ, and thou shalt be saved" (Acts 16:31). If you trust in Jesus, you shall be saved. To the one who says, "I will give myself to Jesus, for I know I want life. I lie down, a corpse, and though I cannot move, I know that when He passes by, He will give me life," go thou! God has something for you. Go and fall before Him. You shall have life bestowed upon you. Go and accept it. For wherever there is a "now," it is of God. The Holy Ghost says, "To day if ye will hear his voice, Harden not your hearts" (Heb. 3:7–8).